PROFESSIONAL LIVES IN AMERICA

*A publication of the Center for the
Study of the History of Liberty in America*

HARVARD UNIVERSITY

PROFESSIONAL LIVES IN AMERICA

STRUCTURE AND ASPIRATION

1750-1850

Daniel H. Calhoun

HARVARD UNIVERSITY PRESS

CAMBRIDGE, MASSACHUSETTS

1965

The Center for the Study of
the History of Liberty in America
is aided by a grant from
the Carnegie Corporation of New York.

TO

MY MOTHER

AND TO THE MEMORY OF

MY FATHER

Foreword

The professions long seem to have provided strategic channels for upward social mobility in the United States. These callings, which required the possession of a recognized skill, offered to some individuals access to positions of high status in expanding communities where skill was always at a premium. To some degree at least, entry into these favored ranks was independent of inherited position or capital. Yet because of their importance the professions were also subject to regulation by the community, either formally through law or informally through the sanctions devised by private associations. The development of these occupations therefore is connected with significant aspects of the history of American liberty.

All such statements must be made in the most tentative and qualified manner because practically nothing is known about the history of the professions in the United States. A considerable anecdotal and biographical literature deals with the lives of individual practitioners; and a good deal has been written about the development of techniques insofar as that touches upon the main lines of intellectual, political, or religious history. But books about the bench and bar of a particular locality or accounts of a prominent lawyer or even analyses of changes in the conception of law only tangentially throw light upon the evolution of the organized structure of the legal profession. The deficiency is equally prominent in the case of teachers, physicians, ministers, and other groups.

To begin to understand the history of the professions, therefore, it was necessary to formulate studies that rested directly upon primary sources. Only thus could a fund of data be assembled that would provide a basis for an outline of the whole subject. Professor Calhoun, whose study of engineers was a pioneer effort in this direction undertook to probe in depth certain critical phases of the history of the professions in the century after 1750. His intention, in the studies presented in this volume, was to elicit from a meticulous examination of specific cases the central problems in the history of the professions.

To do so, he focused upon three different callings as they developed in three different areas of the nation. Medicine, the law, and the ministry were among the earliest to define the status of their practitioners; they involved recognizable skills; and they were associated with superior social position. Furthermore, the development of each raised significant questions about the relationship to the community in which they were exercised. Each was studied in a distinctive setting—medicine in mercantile New York city, law in a region of Tennessee just emerging from the frontier, and the ministry in relatively stable New England.

From his very thoughtful study he has drawn conclusions of the highest importance, not only about the issues of freedom of access, relationships to the state, and regulation, but also about more subtle and less expected developments. His analysis of the tension produced by the efforts to create an exclusive group of practitioners and the proliferation of would-be entrants and the conflicts between the desire for individual distinction and the pressures toward conformity throw light not only upon the historic past but also upon contemporary issues still unresolved.

OSCAR HANDLIN

Preface

The chapters that follow explore a conjunction of circumstance and mood that many observers have seen in nineteenth-century America: the organizational shifts that we know as denominationalism and as the beginnings of a bureaucratic ethos, and the intellectual shifts that we know as increases in objectivity, in professionalism, and in aspiration toward science. These changes were particularly clear in those three "learned professions" that made up the bulk of a class of practical intellectuals: the law, medicine, and the ministry. Until a generation or so ago, there would have been little problem of describing what happened. Science had grown. Men's ability to cooperate and regulate their activities through social policy had also grown. Together, science and social coordination made progress. Now, though, we do not need to take seriously all that has been said by critics of "scientism" and "modernism," in order to feel that that way of perceiving our past is sugary and uncomplicated. Much has been said about emotional and economic bases of knowledge. Much has been said about tensions between individual life and sheltering organization. Much has been said about difficulties in gaining one kind of knowledge without losing another. And much has been said, in however speculative a way, about some relation between patterns of thought and patterns of external life. This developing texture of analysis and speculation has necessarily contributed something of surmise and question to the chapters here, although my intent remains unspeculative and historical.

What I have done is to take three situations in which I sensed some interworking of social structure and professional thought, and to follow leads within each: one situation in which a medical spokesman called for a kind of moratorium on attention to individual achievement; another in which a lawyer formulated a striking but testable account of how his own profession was changing; and one in which a whole group of clergymen, who had identified themselves in terms of a particular polity, found that the pace of the life they followed within that polity was running away from them. This last problem, joining as it does precise definition of changing social structure and explicit commitment to the pure life of the spirit, is the one to which I have given the most attention.

I confess that my initial mood in these explorations was pessimistic. Not all the accomplishments of American romantic literature can argue away the thinness and even vulgarity of nineteenth-century life. Especially in the middle years of the century, before scientific achievements became massive, it seemed as if America had gained little from the difficulties that the learned professions had experienced during the previous century, except a certain caution, a certain provincial decency and inspirationalism. The flatness that both European and American critics found in American culture then is one of the things that need to be explained. Midcentury was not the end of the story, of course; and I am willing to leave open the question of whether the long-range developments then unfolding deserve an optimistic or a pessimistic evaluation.

I want to thank the historians and archivists who helped me find material for these explorations for their aid and hospitality. People at all the depositories mentioned in the notes did much, so that I can only mention the institutions and individuals on whose kindness I drew most often: the New York Academy of Medicine, and Mrs. Alice D. Weaver; the Sumner County Court House, in Gallatin, Tennessee; the Davidson County Court House, in Nashville; the Tennessee State Library and Archives, and Mrs. L. Frank Owsley; the New Hampshire Historical Society, in Concord; the New Hampshire Antiquarian Society, in Hopkinton; the Andover-Harvard Library, and Mr. James Tanis; the New-York Historical Society, and Mr. Wilmer R. Leech; and the Church Historical Society, in Austin, Texas, and Dr. Virginia Nelle Bellamy. For permission to quote from the Murdock Collection of Overton Papers, I am indebted to the kindness of Mr. Stanley F. Horn, president of the Tennessee Historical Society. I am indebted to the Medical Society of the County of New York and Mr. Robert D. Potter for access to the early papers of the Society.

D.H.C.

Contents

Graphs

PROFESSIONAL LIVES IN AMERICA

I

Power, Responsibility, and Style

"The interests" or God: this was the alternative built into a long history of social anxiety about the power of the learned professions, an anxiety that came to a head in America during the years when the country was moving into the experiment of new nationality, then immediately again into the experiment of forced economic development. A physician or a clergyman or a lawyer had certain talents that he placed at the service of those who employed him. Ideally, so the argument ran, he kept his own sensibility to value so keyed that no particular client or congregation could control the way he used his talents. For much of American history, this saving sense of value meant allegiance to God. That alone, people felt, could keep pure those talents that, serving merely human goals, would produce exploitation. If a man of parts faltered in devotion to the highest duty, then those other men who held worldly power—property or the means of coercion—might step in to use him as one of their more subtle instruments. And even if men of power did not act, he would become his own corrupter, a monster whose ability to appropriate the cultural resources of society would enable him to use and discard other men's lives.

Many evangelical sects elaborated this theme in their rhetoric. Baptists, Methodists, and others argued against a "hireling" clergy. Since these groups, like many proper

Congregationalists, often discouraged their members from going to law against each other, and since their preachers sometimes assumed the task of providing medical attention and drugs, this attack on the hireling who took pay for exercising his God-given talents spilled over into an attitude toward all the professions. On one level, the attack was directed against the preacher who simply sought his own gain under the guise of serving an ultimate value; in his crudest form, he was the revivalist with the handy collection plate. More often, the attack operated against the pastor who received a stated salary for serving a particular, settled congregation; it then figured as part of broader assaults on any ecclesiastical polity that permitted such employment. Those who made such attacks were rarely rich or far removed from social dependency; ideas about social subordination either disturbed or offended them. From their point of view, the salaried pastor served the interests of the men of substance who contributed most of his salary; this was true even where smaller voluntary contributions came in from pious Christians who were not wealthy. How could a pastor "divide rightly" the word of God—how, that is, could he give to another man the words with which to articulate the larger pains of existence —if he depended for his own living on men of substance who figured as particulars in the pains with which ordinary men had to cope?

The same split in social allegiances affected the way ordinary people reacted to the medical profession. Practitioners of several different types worked in every community. Some doctors did build large and socially exclusive practices; others contented themselves with patients of middling or lesser consequence. On either level of success, men who were trying to be "regular" physicians—that is, legitimate and orthodox practitioners—attracted those members of the population who were anxious to align themselves with behaviors that might be labeled urbane or English or fashionable. This was not altogether a matter of social class; some reputable people who enjoyed strong familial or communal ties continued to rely on the dosing parson, or on the venerable female relative who acted as something more than nurse. In addition, many lesser people consulted nature healers, or "Indian" doctors, or adherents to some newly devised and eccentric medical system. The heresies that diverged from orthodox medicine during the early part of the nineteenth century did find their usual constituencies in restricted or less than fashionable groups. One brand of nature healing, relying on an authoritative therapeutic manual and a system of local treatment societies, used a quasi-scriptural literalism to tap hostility toward social authority, in much the same way as those religious groups that enlisted resentment against a hireling clergy. Since medical practitioners (as distinct from lawyers and clergymen) dealt little with social issues, the widespread unwillingness to use their services meant only that many people did not participate in the social up-grading or the groping after European standards that seemed to mark the generation around 1800. Only in great moments of irrationality did such alienation become fear of social exploitation—fear that doctors, in the anatomical dissections that were a necessary part of professional training, made a callous, obscene use of the bodies of the poor.

But a fear that lawyers served the interests of wealth against the rest of society was pervasive, plausible, and occasionally justified. Before the Revolution, a Tory who wanted to make a case against certain patriot agitators had only to argue that the patriots served landed gentlemen who wanted to be free of Crown control in order themselves to exploit the people of their neighborhood. Then and later, debtors denounced the lawyer and all the machinery of the law as tools of creditors. Distrust followed even the lawyer who won political office as a popular spokesman: in his overt actions he might keep his promises, but in those technical matters to which his profession was most relevant he might quietly confirm the complaisance of government toward existing wealth and influence.

The image of the professional hireling fed such distrust. As an emotional apprehension, it thrived alongside other kinds of fear that were also directed against professional men but that were not quite consistent with fear of the hireling. In one view, the professional was subservient to social power outside himself, and might become virtuous if he gained freedom of action; in the other, he had power of his own to exploit and injure men. In one respect, fear of the intrinsic power of the professions turned on a realistic and sophisticated view of how society operated: apparent social power, whether proprietary or coercive, was not always real. Just as bureaucrats who prepared agendas and budgets could divert profit to themselves, professional men stood as gatekeepers in a fast-growing, ill-organized society. Men had to pay fees to lawyers and courts to perfect their titles to land. When problems dragged on from term to term in the courts, costs would mount to an unreasonable levy on the total value involved. Antilawyer propaganda stressed the dangers of long suits, especially the danger of getting a property into chancery. Similarly, men feared falling into the hands of a physician who would protract treatment, plausibly and without term.

This particular fear of the toll-collecting professional applied less to the clergy, but only because in an earlier period it had reached such intensity that it had forced a redefinition of the clergy within Protestantism. The taking of fees for performing sacraments and dispensing church favors was one of the abuses that reformers had denounced in papist or prelatical clergy. But the achieved reforms strengthened the very reliance on salary that fed fears of a hireling clergy. Churches in the reformed tradition allowed little scope for the free-lance operator or for the minister not attached to a particular local group. While they did allow a man to receive a fee for preaching outside his own parish or for performing a marriage, they encouraged outside preaching on an exchange basis that avoided payment for services, and they minimized severely those parts of the church service from which a clergyman might derive perquisites. Except in those priestly clergies that never absorbed much of the reformed attitude, the gate-keeping function became largely limited to the ideological (the need for a pastor if men were to attend to all the stated "means of grace") and the political (the obligation in some areas to pay a ministerial tax as one of the consequences of owning property). The efforts to restrict fee taking were, with respect to the clergy, a social arrangement that Americans could take for granted as a legacy from the Old World.

In law and medicine, however, fee taking remained an active problem, especially during the eighteenth and early nineteenth centuries as a preoccupation with formal fee schedules. Costs levied in court cases included lawyers' fees, and men were only just then clarifying the notion that such fees were mere formalities, that lawyers could charge more than the legally assessed fees without being guilty of under-the-counter gouging. Some local judges, as well as other court officials, were still paid by fees alone. Societies of physicians adopted minutely detailed fee tables listing minimums, and hoped to hold their members to

these fees in all ordinary dealings. But whether the schedules were supposed to protect the laity against professional
exploitation, or the professionals against mutual competition, they reflected a need to set bounds and structure
around the toll-taking function of professionals.

Fear of the intrinsic power of professionals went further
than resentment against their ability to take fees. Men
also feared a direct impact of professional techniques. A
lawyer, knowing the law and knowing also the legally
vulnerable points in the economic structure, could act in
his own person, bringing suits for property to which he
had a legal claim but no social right. This danger was reflected in the frequent bar rules forbidding lawyers to
buy up notes in their own names in order to sue for collection. It appeared also in the revulsion against a lawyer
who entered an area of confused land titles, bought up
those that he could get cheaply, then pushed actions against
the other claimants, among whom were included actual
occupants.[1] Of course men felt some admiration for picaresque, successful chicane. They felt more serious ambiv-
alence toward the strenuous techniques used by doctors
and preachers. The lingering fear of anatomical dissection
provided an outlet and extreme expression for other fears
of what doctors could do—fear of the brutal and frequently fatal work of surgeons, and fear of the "heroic"
therapies used by physicians, such as bloodletting, saliva-
ting, purging, and puking. But while men appear to have
avoided the surgeon's knife wherever possible, they seemed
to admire the physician's barbarities. The practitioner who
most impressed an ordinary community was apt to be the
man who came in, administered overdoses of dangerous
chemicals, then was lucky enough to have his patients
pull narrowly and therefore dramatically through to re-

covery.[2] Similarly, many evangelical congregations valued the preacher who could mobilize existential fear and lead it to violent emotional expression. But this greed for intensity was often challenged by men who urged some limit on the use of what clerical jargon called "means." They insisted that the common drugs acted often as deadly poisons, and that doctors should administer only small amounts or should limit their choice of drugs to "natural" substances. Serious medical men, while unimpressed by such arbitrary, rule of thumb approaches to caution, became willing to restrict their use of therapies to those situations in which they had specific grounds for expecting a desired effect. Sober divines accused revivalists of using psychological short cuts to create the symptoms of conversion, thereby risking subsequent depression and dangerous emotional disturbance. On one level, these apprehensions about professional manipulation were directed against means supposed to be fraudulent or ultimately ineffective; but behind all the accusations of fraud simmered an old popular feeling that the learned man, the professional, had found access to some special, genuine knowledge that made him at once useful and dangerous to the rest of humanity.

People feared also that the special techniques might give a monopoly to the professions as such, or to professional in-groups. At the crudest, leaders could obtain laws designed to restrict entry and to regulate the conditions of practice. More subtly, they might convert many of the organized forms of social action—churches, courts, schools, hospitals, and literary societies—into the instruments of a supposed aristocracy of talent. Fear of power worked at the center of such apprehensions; and because the power at issue was not simply proprietary or coercive, those who were fearful tended to expect from the professions some sleight-of-hand—devious and therefore less legitimate than the enforcement of naked subordination.

To such fears, sanity had always a reply. The men involved in the day to day work of the professions could point out undramatic reality: that absolute or overweening power simply did not enter the case; that the professions, like other groups, had certain degrees of power that they could not help exercising; that most of this power was internal, arising from never quite successful efforts that some men made to preserve group cohesion; that a profession must exercise constant care if it was to preserve enough power to act in the public interest. When, during some of the early nineteenth-century epidemics, the body of physicians in a community lacked internal cohesion, it lacked even the power to exert leadership in quarantine measures. When groups of evangelical clergymen failed to maintain discipline among themselves, they had trouble preventing adventurers from using the ministry as a ladder for hypocrisy. Aside from cases of exceptional centralization, such as the American Medical Association in the twentieth century, the power of most professional bodies has tended to dissipate rather than to cumulate. When power has grown, it has been bureaucratic rather than direct. Even the exercise of governmental power on behalf of the professions, as through license legislation, has depended on bureaucratic devices that men easily tire of and forget. Suppressing quacks has been no easier than suppressing sweatshops. Conscientiousness, not ruthlessness, has been the necessary mode of feeling in those who would keep the means of action keyed up to the vigor required by the public interest. And the one justifying object of power has been quality. However much men may have argued about what constituted professional skill, society has always needed men who combined personal ability with training in the best existing subject matter of a profession—and who combined these qualifications with a sense of responsibility to human welfare and to possible improvement in the field. The maintenance of such quality, while depending in part on the prevailing level of intellectual morale in the whole society, has required certain exercises of power: power to keep educational institutions operating at high level, restrictive power to keep unqualified men from entering the profession, fostering power to encourage top-grade performance by those already in, and the last-resort power to throw out the practitioner who might violate obligations to his calling. This argument in justification of power could hardly ignore the fact that all these actions might dampen, or allow the self-seeking to dampen, free competition within the profession; but this too would serve the needs of quality, maintaining a base level of morale by freeing men from pettier preoccupations.

During the latter part of the eighteenth century, the problems that society presented to the professions called for widely varying responses if the different groups were all to raise their levels of performance. The Revolution created as much fluidity as the legal profession needed, throwing forward new sources of legal authority even while it disrupted or depleted the personnel of the bar in many localities. Under such conditions, policies designed to shore up or to order the life of the profession were probably those best calculated to improve the service that lawyers could give the public. Under other conditions, measures to preserve order might instead have hampered service. During the large-scale epidemics of the colonial and early national periods, firm internal discipline could easily have blocked the medical profession from the epidemiological controversy that served it as a crude equivalent to experimentation. True, discipline might have promoted effective quarantine measures; but as long as doctors needed to lose false knowledge from the past, a libertarian regime was the way to greater quality. The freedom of these years permitted some new growth to unconventional schools of medicine that preserved within themselves even more of dogmatism and falsely systematic thinking than persisted within orthodox, regular medicine. But it permitted also the growth within regular medicine of scientific ways of thinking that eventually showed such dogmatism to have been obsolete.

In any period, the amount of actual support that particular social groups gave to quality often differed from the amount of support they thought they gave. All, of course, wanted "good" lawyers and "good" pastors and "good" doctors. They differed, not simply in their standards of what was good, but in how far they favored impersonal quality, apart from those characteristics in a professional man that induced emotional trust. Upper groups presumably gave greater favor to high-level performance, associating it at times with their tendency to label themselves as "the quality." Whether such groups understood a profession well enough to appreciate performance was another matter. The landed gentleman who made it his duty to know some law probably had as sound ideas as any layman could of the virtues in lawyers who came his way. But the urban gentleman of merely literary culture had no basis on which to judge a physician except manner, plausibility, and compatibility; and he had few standards except the oratorical on which to judge a clergyman. Perhaps both the upper and the lower extremes of society judged the professional on a standard of social closeness— is he one of us?—while middling groups, rooted in nothing quite so deeply as in education and self-improvement, measured quality in a more detached way.

The problems of interpreting the varying attitudes toward ministers in the Great Awakening seem to point toward this way of distinguishing between groups. In the earlier stages of the movement, intrinsic pietistic motives led men of all social levels to support the call for vital religion and for a truly "converted" ministry; the significant cleavages were those between men of different temperament, on each social level. But as the Awakening became more intense, and as itinerant preachers attacked more harshly those ministers whose qualifications were merely intellectual, dominant groups in the laity and in the clergy re-formed a more consistent defense against the attack. For many of them, decency and order became the prime marks of an acceptable minister. What proper society interpreted as intellect could itself become a conventional badge of acceptability, while unguarded piety began to seem common or vulgar. The individuals who best managed to preserve an allegiance to both intellect and piety at once were apt to be those who lacked secure social ties.

The identity of groups that gave lasting support to full professional standards was unstable, depending often on short-term conditions. If a difference between liberal and conservative temperaments seems at times a useful distinction between ministers who favored new revival measures and those who resisted such measures, it does not justify any picture of "liberals" or "conservatives" acting in relation to professional reform movements. Neither is there much lasting reliability in a cleavage between "best people" and "muckers," or in its modern equivalent, that between urban reason and agrarian unreason. The apparent

successors of workingmen who resisted professional regulation as a monopoly device in one generation might accept
it as an incident to the welfare state in another generation;
much depended on whether they sensed professional men
as alien or as types of their own children's future advancement. All kinds of people could like practical results more
than they feared power.

But the American desire to be practical has often relieved men from seeing real, painful social cleavages. It has
rather assured all groups that they stood at one time or
other for the essence of what finally emerged. Sane, practical men can thus miss any memory of those brief junctures
of conflict in which social groups revealed themselves.
Falsely simple though such junctures are, they are intellectually useful when they occur in professional life, opening
a sight line from the technical sphere of professionalism
into the general world of social feeling.

Inconsistency in which social group really favored the
use of power to promote quality is less important than the
fact that the prevailing level of applied power has shifted
from generation to generation. Antiauthoritarian arguments may allow much greater scope to legitimate authority in one period than in another, and the defenders of
power may vary in what they allow as necessary individual
freedom. The existence of some assumed level of authority,
around which argument fluctuates, helps make the distinct
social "tone" or "style" of a period. And the wide distribution of views on either side of such a level at any one time
allows some observers to ignore substantial shifts in the
center of social tone. A community-oriented style, accepting gracefully the use of authority to promote group interests in American societies, has had its important exponents
in most generations. A liberal style, advocating freedom of
action for the large number of independent and substantial

units in American society, has had its exponents. One might pick and choose evidence to show that either one has dominated the whole span of American life. But the two styles do define the kind of shift that Americans experienced as they moved from the colonial years into the fullness of the nineteenth century. Communal values and action yielded before a growing market orientation. Not all communities, not all individuals, participated equally in this shift. It was no blocklike change from The Traditional Society to The Liberal Society. In the eighteenth century, communal standards probably meant more in rural New England villages than in any other part of the country, even though they had other kinds of reality in the single-sect communities or even in the looser county societies, farther south. These standards probably meant least in commercial towns of all regions, despite the municipal regulations that those towns tried to enforce. Thus much of the shift toward the nineteenth-century style was a matter of a continuing, growing spill of town standards over into the countryside. This spill characterized both the liberalizing trend and certain developments that seemed to resist the trend.

Consider, for instance, medical life. The typical early rural neighborhood rarely had more than two or three accessible practitioners;[3] through their monopoly position such men dominated the community market for professional services, and only in the larger towns was legal regulation really necessary to keep order in a larger professional group. Then, as the rural areas grew more populous and more like towns in social structure, additional doctors took up practice, until the structure of the local profession began to acquire a more fluid, liberal, townish character; but this very change at first led some rural areas to use regulatory measures that they earlier had hardly considered. Different communities acted in different ways within the larger shift, producing a wide scatter of kinds of change. The texture of social change in America, far from being crude, displayed a flurried, complex surface.

If, like social change of most kinds, shifts in professional life were a matter of degree rather than of sudden leaps, then explorations of professional development may legitimately use methods suited to degree—may seek measures that "quantify" stylistic change. The substance of such development was mostly qualitative. It involved techniques of practice and patterns of scholarship. It involved the sense of group cohesion or the suspicion that professional men sometimes felt toward each other. It involved the kind of trust that laymen had in practitioners, as also the sense of security that practitioners felt in their careers. It involved the question of whether a particular professional context provided discipline and responsibility, or whether it gave scope to individual ambition and spontaneity. And it involved the whole pattern of dependent or divergent relations between American life and the professional traditions of Europe. But the fact that change has had important qualitative aspects has not, in certain other areas of American life, precluded measurement. Much, for instance, of the shift in business life that took place in the late nineteenth and early twentieth centuries was qualitative or stylistic. It involved techniques of influence, patterns of deference, the sense of security or of panic, even the degree of cosmopolitanism or provincialism in business attitudes. Nevertheless, some kinds of measurement have provided indexes of change in these qualitative aspects. This is part of what statisticians are up to when they devise measures of corporate concentration. For some things, of course, there are no satisfactory measures: witness the attempts to assess the creativity of scientists or engineers by the number of patents they take out. But as long as change is complex and varied, measurement may at least restrict the oversimplification entailed in bare ideological categories such as "liberal" and "communal."

The importance of matters of degree was built into American professional life from the beginning by the kinds of ideological formulation that men brought with them when they crossed the water. Just as the ministry, the learned vocation that survived when society dispensed with others, was primary among the professions, so the core of these formulations lay in theology. Grace, almost everyone admitted, came ultimately from God, and came to none except as an expression of God's sovereign will. But on the immediate scene some things that men did seemed to help the intervention of grace: praying, receiving the sacraments, listening to sermons, reading pious literature. Most of these "means of grace" involved action by a professional man. The high achievements of theology centered on reconciling God's sovereignty with man's freedom, the necessity of grace with the employment of means, pious intensity with professional order. Every major theological view, Anglican as well as Puritan, took these problems into account, although Puritanism with its sense of bargain between God and man kept such problems closer to the foreground.

Similar intellectual reconciliations characterized the other professions. The concept of orthodoxy, which meant adherence to a hardly won balance between divergent ideas, not just a submission to arbitrary rule, had its place in medicine. On the one hand, learned physicians acquired from the past certain systems that established the outlines of medical truth. On the other, they lived with the possibility of stepping up the impressiveness of their own performances, either by administering ever larger doses of heroic drugs or by introducing novel therapies drawn empirically from nature and practice. Medical propriety recognized the possibility that doctors would find new, empirical therapies; lacking means of assessing the new, it insisted that the new be somehow compatible with authoritative, received theory. In legal practice, standards of eloquence followed somewhat the same lines as standards of pulpit technique. Direct emotional impact, savoring of free grace, was important; so were discipline, a respect for authorities, and a sense of form. In one kind of adjustment between these competing standards, the professional was presumed to have so mastered and absorbed both the matter in his field and the issues in the problem at hand that a formed, efficacious language would flow from him as soon as he let go the barriers to speech. In all the learned fields, some such adjustment coped not only with the competition between training and intensity as standards of professional quality, but also with dangers from an undisciplined use of means. It provided a frame in advance for that very scatter of attitudes and styles that became the substance of later complexity.

The need to impose control on professional techniques figured especially in the profession that was defined by its use of really dangerous, coercive means. If Americans only occasionally thought of the military as one of the learned professions, the infrequency with which they included it in lists of the professions[4] signalized the extent to which they feared it. To the English fear of authoritarianism in the form of a standing army they added an ever fresh fear of the extraordinary individual who might use military power in ways that no one could predict. At the same time, these two fears operated against each other. Men who most feared a professional army argued that skilled leadership would be provided instead by inspired, natural genius, while men who argued for formal military training believed that natural genius offered less skill than it did danger. Americans came closest to an organizational solution to this dilemma in their emphasis on the militia, in which ordinary members elected the professional leaders in much the same way that vestries or church memberships called pastors. This organizational form provided a frame for the practical responsibility that was needed by all those ideologies of reconciliation that informed professional life. Holding professional men to account was a main function of militia elections, just as it was one of the major functions served by church councils and presbyteries, whatever the formal authority of such bodies. At least in the generations around 1800, the possibility of bringing practitioners to book for ethical violations seemed a central function toward which new medical organizations regularly gravitated. For military men, often for lawyers, and occasionally even for physicians, the code of honor that issued in duels provided an additional means of holding men responsible for their own conduct. A complementary relation seemed to hold between these two institutions, the disciplinary council and the duel; a professional group that used one had that much less need for the other.

The duel was a casual symbol of a wider, more important emphasis in American life, that on individual assertiveness and individual responsibility. Europeans might have thought it odd for sober bourgeois lawyers and even doctors to adopt the code of honor. But legal and medical practice, because they had found little place in seventeenth-century America and had then been resorbed into the sphere of clerical function, had developed little institutional base on which professional life could grow at the time when lawyers and doctors began to appear again in increasing numbers, over the middle of the eighteenth century. Although medical life began to settle into the communal way, ambitious individuals sought in both law and medicine a kind of distinction that had never attached to the proper clerical career. In these areas, Americans were often ready either to do without professional services or to give patronage to some man whom orthodox practitioners would label an adventurer. The very absence of strong institutions meant that, when some doctors and lawyers and military men began imitating European forms in the latter part of the eighteenth century, they often filled the lack quite rapidly with associations, schools, doctrines, publications, and professional codes—all of which became a brittle crust concealing much popular indifference to such forms.

The several modes of action that carried over from the colonial period—whether of continuing clerical order, of "American" self-service and individualism, or of the newer moves to build a cosmopolitan culture—were vulnerable to disruption because of their variety and inconsistency. Those practices by which responsibility was enforced ran often against competing standards, such as the antimonopoly sentiment that challenged medical fee tables. The ideologies that reconciled intensity with order ran out into a balancing of considerations that was too complex for most men. It took a careful mind to appreciate the allowances for growth contained within the medical systems that weighed on orthodox late-eighteenth-century practice. It took taste to direct a union between spontaneity and chaste learning into any use of eloquence as a professional means. And it certainly would have required high intelligence to keep alive the covenant theology of Puritanism. These intellectual adjustments, though they each included some kind of order as only one of the reconciled elements, became themselves a higher level of discipline and therefore a reinforced instrument of the communal style. But as sectarianism and vocational specialization continued to increase, separate groups tended to provide special havens for each among the divergent emphases that earlier ideology had reconciled. With the bonds of reconciliation dissolving, the danger grew that neither the specialists in inspiration nor the specialists in formal training would achieve the subtlety and complex seriousness that earlier ways had demanded. This danger American intellectuals—meaning, for the most part, American professionals—faced as they moved toward national life.

Fear of Individuality

JOHN W. FRANCIS AND THE
NEW YORK MEDICAL COMMUNITY

Mass culture in America has never really deserved extreme
fear or extreme denunciation. Uniformity has had many
flaws—gaps through which individuals could push petty
eccentricity or large accomplishment. And something
within popular values has inhibited even the mass American from denying outright the value of individual
achievement. True, he has at one time or another demanded a leveling in access to public jobs, or in the
granting of academic honors; but the particular Americans
who have made these demands have been potential recipients of favor or have been the sponsors of recipients.
If an American dissents bluntly from individualism, he is
being odd. When, therefore, a leader in one of the learned
professions takes a public stand against individualism,
something has gone askew.

This is what happened in the New York medical community in the winter of 1847-48, in two public addresses
delivered by John W. Francis.[1] Francis was speaking on
behalf of a new, intellectually ambitious society, the New
York Academy of Medicine, which physicians had organized to elevate the standing of their profession and to
fight the forces of quackery and medical heresy. He spoke
at a time when doctors were organizing similar societies
in other communities, and when they were also organizing

the American Medical Association.[2] He spoke to the particular need of New Yorkers and New York physicians; but he also spoke to the needs of all American doctors at the middle of the nineteenth century.

Francis seemed the logical person to defend individuality. Attacking it instead, he expressed feelings at odds with his surface traits. Although a man of prudence, abhorring controversy, he had made a long, idiosyncratic career under the sponsorship of David Hosack, who had created a one-leader medical faction and maintained it through the professional politics of a generation. Francis' family had some money but no social consequence, and he had spent a little time as a printer's apprentice. He began his medical study in 1807 under Hosack, whom he later described as forming, with De Witt Clinton and Bishop Hobart, the "tripod" upholding New York society. He took his medical degree at the College of Physicians and Surgeons, then studied in Great Britain, where according to one observer he acquired manners and speech that set him off from New Yorkers. Soon after Francis finished his studies, Hosack took him on as partner. After a few more years, Francis was regularly one of the professors on every medical faculty that Hosack headed. Whenever Hosack found himself embattled in a dispute, whether in matters of education or journalism or sanitary regulation or etiological theory, Francis was there fighting on the same side. Francis was the follower, to be sure; he never achieved the originality or the cantankerousness of Hosack. Yet after Hosack's death Francis became known as the eccentric physician, adhering to old styles of doctors' dress and manner, and defending the heroic therapy that had prevailed in the early part of the century.[3]

The circumstances of his two speeches defined him as making a concession to collective values that were not quite his own. While the Academy excluded from membership all irregular practitioners, whether homeopaths, botanics, or nostrum venders, it welcomed all respectable, regular physicians. It thus included many against whom Francis or Hosack had fought during the previous generation. The first steps toward organizing the Academy were taken toward the end of 1846. When formally organized early in 1847, the Academy elected as its president John Stearns, a politically minded regular physician who had long worked for professional standards but who in earlier years had resisted the influence of the Hosack-Francis group.[4] Stearns, however, was the least of the obnoxious associates to whom Francis had to accommodate himself. In 1826, strong pressures had forced the whole Hosack group to resign from the faculty of the College of Physicians and Surgeons; they had been replaced as the faculty by a younger clique, many of whom were now members of the Academy. The bitterness was not yet dead in 1847; in the 1850's, some of the same men were to be accused in public of having worked for decades to destroy the practice of Francis and doctors like him.[5]

If the grouping of personalities within the Academy signaled a suppression of individual differences, the physical setting of Francis' first address bespoke an appeal to the popular mind. For the meeting the Academy hired the Broadway Tabernacle, which had been built eleven years earlier as a church for the revivalist Charles G. Finney; it was the largest auditorium in New York. When the church fell into financial troubles in the 1840's, it began renting its building out to anyone who wanted to use it for purposes not sinful. Lecturers, reformers, demonstrators of wonders, musical performers—all were accepted as offering clean money, and the Tabernacle became

the great popular platform. Here the Academy of Medicine came when it had a case to present to the public,
and here a reported 10,000 people came to hear the
Academy spokesman.[6]

Much of what Francis said in his Tabernacle speech
was anecdote, entertaining an audience with reminiscent
praise of physicians. But in both this speech and the later
one, his main purpose was political: to argue against
dangerous ideas about the medical profession, and to
formulate a conception of the profession that physicians
and public should adopt. He argued in general terms
against the more serious medical heresies of the day, but
avoided giving them much explicit publicity. He argued,
too, against the notion that the profession was unprogres-
sive, unwilling to accept new ideas. On this point he sum-
moned up example after example of advances recently
made. And in the first of his two speeches he coupled this
progressive medicine with the value of individual effort:

The influence of this Academy, it is hoped, will contribute
in no small measure to destroy that casuistry which sometimes
insinuates itself in discussions among minds of limited grasp,
on the supposed ultra-conservative tendency in medicine. It
will unfurl the banner of philosophy, and in the march for
truth, allow every one to pursue the path he deems best for its
attainment. Free discussion will be cherished in good faith, as
the light thus emanating imparts the purest lustre, and detects
error in its most hidden recess. It will exult in discovery . . .
It will offer the right hand of fellowship to the honest and
intelligent seeker as well as to the man of established attain-
ments. It will cheer on the lonely enthusiast, whose intellectual energies are concentrated upon the analysis of facts, and
heartily encourage the assiduous observer, who is never weary
of collecting the materials for induction . . . It is the part
of a narrow and feeble spirit to suffer any limits to aspira-
tions; and while the rational physician will never proceed
an iota beyond the boundaries of scientific authority, he will

be ever on the alert to detect every dawning star in the horizon of his art.[7]

Good enough. Francis took his stand with the angels of individual achievement. The only difficulties were "scientific authority"—an odd phrase—and his conception of what the "lonely enthusiast" takes as his task: "analysis of facts" and "collecting the materials for induction." Elsewhere in the address, Francis denounced "showy speculation" and "inane disquisition." He said, "It cannot be disputed that the widest difference exists between that wise conservatism which advances with cautious induction by known truths, to others still hidden, and that restless spirit of innovation, which in order to secure its ends, spurns all control, and rejects the clearest demonstrations established by our predecessors for the best interests of man."[8] Much of this was the bluff positivist spirit, allowing no room for the slightest leap of theory; and much was simple prudence. But there was more. Francis took space in his discourse to tick off the accomplishments of local medical men, mentioning only dead physicians and the living president Stearns. Introducing his remarks on men recently dead, he apologized to those who knew more than he did about particular individuals, then added, "Diversity of opinion as to special merits may exist among us; the aggregate worth which they embodied gives the cheering consolation, that New-York has steadily advanced in her professional career; that medicine has in these later days flourished with increased renown, in all its departments, and that she has furnished her full quota of elevated minds, cultivated understandings, benevolent hearts, and real practical disciples, to grace the noble faculty of healing."[9] Before launching into rhetoric, Francis thus let slip his antithesis:

"diversity of opinion" and "special merits" were suspect; only "aggregate worth" consoled.

In his inaugural, delivered on a more strictly professional occasion, Francis shifted the balance of his themes. He still urged the cause of research, insisting that the Academy not be a mere union against homeopaths. He told of an incident thirty years earlier, when his preceptor Hosack had returned home late to greet some guests who included Gouverneur Morris: " 'Mr. Morris, I have been detained with some friends, who together this evening have founded a Philosophical Society' . . . 'Well, well, that's no difficult matter,' rejoined Morris, 'but pray, Doctor, where are the philosophers?' The Doctor was quite embarrassed. And what is the moral of this anecdote? That something more than confederation is requisite; our earnestness must be made palpable by action; work must be done; investigation must be prosecuted; results must be presented."[10]

Results, practicality, "the inductive system of philosophy": "The age and the community in which we live demand reality." The juncture between group values and intellectual diffidence became tight. The Academy was not based on "intolerance" or favor to a privileged few: "If that proper standard be sustained, touching human conduct in the affairs of men, that he who renders greatest services is actually the greatest man, mere accidental or official nominal distinction is lost, the true principle of rank is recognized, and our deference is bestowed according to a determined law of the social compact."[11] The Academy met "on the platform of perfect equality"— "Let is not, therefore, even be whispered, that we suffer by distracted counsels, or from jealousy, or from an acrimonious tenacity of individual opinion or belief. Reason is to be left free to encounter inquiry, because truth is secured by so wise and philosophic a procedure. Nor shall a vain-glorious reflection upon special merit ever obtrude itself to mar that grateful alliance to which we are all pledged one to another."[12] Here the spokesman for an intellectual profession urged individual study yet rejected individual opinion, individual belief, individual theory, and individual merit.[13]

The contrast raises two questions. Why did the New York medical community come to regard individual action as dangerous? And why, even if they feared laissez faire in their social and economic affairs, did physicians assume that the danger applied also in thought and learning and expression?

The answers lie in the pattern through which the medical community had developed for over fifty years. During the latter part of the eighteenth century, some individuals and groups began working to build the strength and morale of the New York profession. But while they pushed their efforts, they also wrangled in a way exceeding what public and profession alike had long accepted as "doctors' quarrels." They differed over cognitive matters, such as etiological and therapeutic doctrine. They fought over the profits and prestige to be had from controlling medical education. They quarreled (or they accused each other of quarreling) over patients, competing in an ordinary way or sniping at each others' reputations. And they argued over organization itself—whether the profession should constitute a corporate entity, whether such a body should admit only select members, and who the select members might be. Lines of cleavage appeared: between entrenched doctors and marginal practitioners, between individual leadership and group consensus, between exclusive small groups and inclusive large ones, between the students of one faction leader and the students of another. Since these lines of cleavage did not coincide, doctors who represented a stand taken on one kind of issue found allies by constructing appeals to doctors who for the moment felt stronger about a different issue. Such alliances were not stable. Each joining of issues created more antagonism than it resolved. The story of these controversies will explain why doctors reacted against individualism, and may suggest an explanation of how they came to implicate the intellectual life in their social fears.

In 1750, the medical community had had only the loosest organization. If doctors met as a group they probably did so as cognoscenti, more than in a narrowly professional character. Change began in the early 1760's. By that time, gatherings of physicians were becoming more clearly medical.[14] By that time, too, Americans trained in British medical schools were returning to New York, seeing in the medical community a whole that might be raised to Old World standards through the creation of community-wide institutions. Several among them, while waiting for practice, gave lectures on medical subjects to young doctors. Samuel Bard promoted a full-scale medical school, and was disappointed only that Philadelphia physicians succeeded by a short margin in making their city the first in the colonies to boast such an institution. Sir James Jay sought to create a school under his own chieftainship, and his mere scheme, although unrealized, blocked the ambitions of another man, who hoped to give lectures as an individual. Each plan for establishing a school reflected either an individual doctor's failure to find enough to do or his ambition to command a major practice in the small city. In the case of Samuel Bard, such concern was needless. His father, John Bard, had been practicing successfully in New York and planned to turn patients over to his son. Jay's promotional efforts failed, but Samuel Bard's succeeded, uniting as they did his British training and the backing of established local physicians. By 1770, this combined leadership produced three institutions amounting to a medical community: the New York Hospital, the medical faculty of King's College, and the local medical association.[15]

This last, the medical association, did not achieve much formal organization before the Revolution. A more formal group, encouraged by the participation of military surgeons, flourished during the British occupation.[16] The broken succession re-emerged after the Revolution in the so-called Medical Society of the State of New York, an unofficial organization that took its membership from the city, not from the state as a whole. At first, almost all physicians with any pretension to prominence belonged to the Society. From this group came most of the Faculty of Physic of Columbia College. From this group came medical staff for the New York Hospital, which was limping back into existence during these years. And it was to the Medical Society that the managers of the New York Dispensary gave the right of naming its physicians when it was established in 1791. The Society took the lead in setting a fee schedule to which respectable physicians should conform, and it assumed that it could speak for the profession in recommending surgeons to the Army and Navy.[17] Until 1791, the only sign of weakness in the medical establishment was the anti-dissectionist riot of 1788, when physicians depended on respectable people for physical protection.[18] But this showed only that the group had a narrow base of social support, not that it suffered from internal dissension.

In 1791, two fissures appeared. First, some elements in the community made serious demands that the Dispensary

deprive the Medical Society of its right to nominate physicians. While not charging the Society with anything
more than a lack of absolutely pure motives in its charity,
the dissenters did assume for virtually the first time that
respectable physicians could be found outside the entrenched group. Second, an ambitious physician seceded
from the established group. Nicholas Romayne, who had
been a member of the Columbia Medical Faculty during
the 1780's, set up his own school. Among the teachers he
recruited was Sir James Jay, who had been frustrated in
his own plans for medical leadership in the 1760's. In the
later recollection of one physician, the established group
feared that Romayne planned to draw all medical students
into his orbit, at the same time forcing other physicians
out of practice in the city, leaving him the "Consulting
Physician General" at the head of a subservient profession.[19] Whatever was the exact case, they did block Romayne's project by intervening with the Board of Regents,
who exercised a general supervision over education in
New York State, and persuading them not to sponsor it.
He tried to operate his school as an affiliate of Rutgers,
then left medical life to shuttle between Britain and
America until 1797, when he entered Blount's conspiracy
to promote British influence in the Southwest.

A third split in the New York medical community
developed in 1794, possibly because the Republican views
of some physicians clashed with the Federalist temperament of the older group. During 1794 the Medical Society
was reorganized, with many fewer members. A rival society soon appeared, calling itself the College of Physicians. During the yellow fever epidemic of 1795, the two
groups disagreed bitterly on how to advise the city officials.
Although the College took an antialarmist line that was
much more likely to win support from commercial in-

terests, the Society convinced officials and the public that all physicians outside its membership were negligible, second-rate men. The College therefore soon dropped from sight, but its threat may have prompted the Society to use a very different tactic when the next medical split developed. In 1802, when a group of outside physicians organized the Physical Society, the Medical Society moved quickly to establish an informal alliance with the new group, communicating to it the system of "etiquette" that governed relations among its own members, and electing the secretary of the new group to the Medical Society.

Such an alliance only postponed troubles. During the 1790's, either the ambition of a determined individual or the dissatisfaction of excluded physicians could challenge the prescriptive position of the old medical community, especially by making common cause with marginal practitioners. And north of the city there loomed the largest single group of excluded physicians: the whole upstate profession, of whom the Medical Society had presumed to act as virtual representatives.

By 1805 both the Medical Society and some newer, more obscure upstate groups were becoming unhappy with existing law, which provided for licensing medical practice on about the same basis as theatrical performances. The Society wanted either a strict licensing statute or, for itself, legal incorporation and recognition. The upstate group had a different problem: migration from New England into northern New York had brought an assortment of ill-educated practitioners. The better educated among the Yankees found a common interest with physicians already there, in setting up some standard of medical respectability. Groups from Saratoga, Montgomery, and Washington counties, with John Stearns among their active leaders, asked the legislature to incorporate societies in their counties. In 1806 the legislature enacted a new law that went beyond their request, meeting also (after a fashion) the demands from the city. It amounted to a general incorporation law, authorizing physicians in each county to organize a society with corporate status. Each would have the right to examine and license physicians within its bounds, and all would send representatives to a state society.[20]

This law suited better the wishes of the upstate men than it did those of the old Medical Society, which objected to the requirement that all legal practitioners become members of the county society; this conflicted with the exclusive, small-group attitude of the establishment. Some of the members of the older New York Medical Society hesitated to accept the law, which was in fact permissive, not mandatory. But if they abstained from the new effort, other physicians might go right ahead and form the county society anyway, thus becoming a rival organization operating with legal sanction. Besides, the new society would have some features that the older professional groups wanted. Reluctantly, the Medical Society of New York voted to disband, yielding its identity to the new Medical Society of the County of New York.

For its pains, it suffered a rebuff in the initial organization of the County Society. On July 1, 1806, the County Society elected as its first president Nicholas Romayne, who had recently returned from his travels. Romayne's election produced a test of whether the two kinds of dissent from the old establishment could coalesce, a test of whether the assertive individualist could provide leadership to the marginal members of the medical community. At first Romayne called for "liberality."[21] Under his presidency, the Society disavowed one key policy of the old Medical Society, that of establishing a fee schedule to which all physicians in the city were to conform. And he identified himself with a plan whereby all the members were to seek incorporation also as a parallel group, the College of Physicians and Surgeons, which would then operate a medical school in competition with the old and moribund Columbia Medical Faculty.

But the role of aggressive medical leadership seems to have demanded in this situation a species of treachery. Romayne, first, deliberately failed his leadership test. Given the task of lobbying for incorporation of the College of Physicians and Surgeons, he went to Albany. When he returned, he reported that he had not presented the legislature with the Society's petition because he did not want to excite public reaction against the physicians' quarrel—by which he presumably meant that he did not want to meet head-on the hostile lobbying of the Columbia Medical Faculty. Instead he had applied to the Regents, who had in law the power to grant the M.D. degree, and the Regents had obliged by creating a College of Physicians and Surgeons. Every member of the County Society was a "member" of the new College, but control remained in the hands of the Regents or of the men the Regents named as professors. Nor surprisingly, the Regents named Romayne president. Romayne clearly expected that the County Society would not like this arrangement. He worked with the State Society to obtain regulations limiting the power of county societies: he obtained for the College of Physicians and Surgeons a direct relation to the state group equivalent to the status of a county society—and he asked the New York County Society to accept these moves as wholesome and liberal, designed to curb selfish interests.[22]

The County Society felt betrayed—a feeling in which Romayne and others were soon to join them. Among the men whom Romayne secured for his faculty was the young David Hosack, who had been a protégé of Samuel Bard, former dean of the Columbia Medical Faculty. After a few years Hosack accepted a chair at Columbia, too; some of the Columbia men apparently thought he was coming over to their interest, for they denounced him for treachery when he swung definitely back to the College of Physicians and Surgeons after another short period. Actually Hosack was participating in an elaborate series of maneuvers whereby the College and the Columbia Medical Faculty were amalgamated, Bard became the new president of the College, Romayne was left again to run a private school for a few years, and some of the Columbia Medical Faculty were left out in their dudgeons. During all this, Hosack and others argued mightily that New York could not have a sound medical community except with a single, noncompetitive medical school.[23]

For a time the old community medical establishment seemed alive again, yet on a new level that was neither the generalized medical community of the County Society nor the traditional leadership of the former Medical Society. It may be significant that the years in which Hosack arranged the amalgamation were pretty much the same years that he lobbied the sale of his Botanic Gardens to the state. After that, he devoted much less of his teaching time to botany and the materia medica, and much more to the professionally central subjects of clinical medicine and the theory and practice of physic. In Romayne's example Hosack had sensed the kind of role that had survival value. Following it, and usurping Romayne's position, he cut himself loose from the kind of medical leadership that relied on social position, informal sanctions, and a generalized or gentlemanly approach to knowledge. He became no less conservative, no less concerned to preserve the professional leadership of his own group; but he led that group into a more vocational mode of gaining its ends.[24]

The clash between community consciousness and individual ambition appeared again in 1819, when the County Society, led by some younger physicians who were themselves ambitious to become medical teachers, attacked the College of Physicians and Surgeons for excessive tuition costs and lax standards. Hosack defended the College with civic-sounding arguments, but at the same time he tried to negotiate a secret deal through which he and John W. Francis would secede from New York altogether and join one of the Philadelphia medical schools.[25]

Hosack in turn lost power in medical education, but to a group, rather than to a new individual leader. Some younger physicians of the 1820's, thrown together partly by their work in the New York Hospital but including also certain men who had clashed with Hosack in 1819, organized a secret fraternity, Kappa Lambda, as an expression of their common interest. When the attack on the College of Physicians and Surgeons came to a head in 1826, men from this group replaced Hosack and his associates as the faculty.[26] Although Hosack continued to operate his own school until 1839 as the Rutgers Medical Faculty, the new group retained sole access to official privilege; degrees from their college counted as licenses without further examination by a medical society.

One thing all these factions—Romayne, or Hosack, or Kappa Lambda—did agree on: they did not like the 1806 requirement that the County Society accept all legal practitioners as members.[27] Even under Romayne's early liberal regime, the County Society sought legal advice from its counselor, Thomas Addis Emmett; Emmett declared that the Society did not have to accept any new members who did not conform to its bylaws, and the Society proceeded to load the bylaws with provisions to discourage unwanted members.[28] After Romayne lost favor, those who succeeded him as leaders kept right on passing regulations to evade nonselective membership.[29] In 1818 the more inclusive-minded physicians, probably including some upstate men, were influential in drafting a new medical law that cut away at the techniques of evasion. The New York County Medical Society consulted Emmett again, and he provided them with new devices based partly on defects in the new law and partly on the notion that no law could force individuals to join a corporation.[30] Emmett's new techniques were soon threatened by pressures for expansion. By 1825, applications for membership in the County Society increased sharply. Many of them had to be accepted, and the implications of wide membership appeared at once: in 1825, doctors in the County Society brought against each other a rash of charges of violating the code of medical ethics. As members grew more numerous in the late 1820's the resistance to inclusiveness weakened. Hosack was staying away from Society meetings because of educational quarrels; and John Stearns, now a recent migrant from upstate, was becoming active in the County Society.[31]

The State Society, meanwhile, continued to back the liberal, inclusive policy to which Stearns and even Romayne had appealed at the outset of the society system. In 1817, for instance, after the County Society adopted a new fee table, the State Society forbade any county society to do this. This prohibition probably represented the effort of upstate physicians to prevent the medical economy of the city from hardening into a cartel that the aspiring migrant from the country could not enter.[32]

It did not sanction the kind of individualism that issued in "doctors' quarrels," for at that time, New York physicians were rediscovering one old device for confining such quarrels through society action. In 1823 the State Society adopted a code of ethics. This code reaffirmed the decision against fee tables while suggesting that no decent physician would either charge too much or cheapen his services by charging too little. The underlying theme of the code, though, was opposition to individual differences. On instructions from the Society, the drafting committee gave special attention to consultation—in other words, to the formal process within which physicians could easily work damage to each other's interests. The kind of consultation that prevailed then and that the committee sought to regulate was still that in which one general practitioner gave moral support to another; in the committee's view, specialization could only indicate "personal or interested motives." Professing to recognize the purely individual, real differences between physicians, the code still betrayed great fear of competitive devices:

There is no difference between physicians but such as results from their personal talents, medical acquirements, or their experience; and the public, from the services they receive, are the natural judges of these intellectual advantages. In all probability, every good physician would receive a merited share of patronage, were there not many who usurp a portion through artful insinuation, and slanders of others, or combinations against, or improper interferences with the more worthy practitioner. Any physician thus molested or injured is justifiable in applying for redress to the County Medical Society to which he is attached.[33]

The appeal to liberal ideas had run into its inevitable problem: was a truly liberal policy one that removed restriction, even from the activities of those whose advantages permitted them to eclipse other, competing operators, or was it one that used restriction to preserve the vigor and approximate equality of many middling competitors?

As far as the medical organizations of the city were concerned, the unavoidable test of liberality was implied in their very existence. How many physicians, in what ratio to the whole medical community, and of what defined types, should each include in its membership? Should each adopt an inclusive or an exclusive policy? If exclusive, should it try to define exclusion to mean ostracism from medical respectability or only a denial of favor and fellowship?

In 1827 the proponents of inclusiveness secured a new law ordering the county societies to take in all legal practitioners. While some elements in the New York County Society sought new ways of evasion,[34] they had no immediate success, and the Society continued to grow. Soon indications appeared that the opponents of inclusiveness had known what they were talking about. A new and more serious round of ethics cases came before the Society.[35] In 1832, one doctor used an argument that revealed the dynamics of the situation. Accused of stealing a patient, he countered by saying that he had not known that his accuser belonged to the Society; obviously, a nonmember deserved no courtesies.[36] Even if the defendant's asserted ignorance was false, he at least assumed that one doctor could plausibly claim that he did not know whether a competitor belonged to the County Society. As recently as 1820, the Society had had only 86 members, with attendance at meetings rarely higher than a third of that.[37] By 1831, attendance alone had climbed to 138 at an election meeting, and total membership may have been larger yet. Membership was growing far past the size within which men could know even their enemies.

Growth also brought something more than the old reshuffling of who belonged to what medical faction. It changed, twice, the very issues on which the primary factional lines were drawn. Until 1829, the main cleavage was educational: Columbia against Romayne, Romayne against Hosack, Hosack against the Kappa Lambda group. From about 1829 on, more and more of the new members crowding into the County Society had no ties to any existing faction. Some were marginal physicians who wanted to attack all special privilege in medicine. Some were moderate reformers, like Stearns. Some were homeopaths with Germanic notions that the Society should undertake a far stricter system of examinations than ever before.[38] Some were the remnants of the Hosack group. During the early 1830's, various combinations of these elements won several Society elections. Although in 1831 they pushed a plan for a Society-sponsored medical school somewhat like the originally contemplated College of Physicians and Surgeons, their aims were in general ideological rather than educational—broadly reformist, attacking privilege and monopoly.[39] At first, all reform elements agreed on attacking Kappa Lambda. Then in 1831 and 1832, the more determined reformers gained strength, pushing their program with such vigor that meetings became noisy and bitter.[40] In November 1831 the Society made its formal attempt to establish the New York School of Medicine, with Stearns and at least one former Rutgers professor among the lecturers.[41]

The school never really got going, and the moderates became increasingly uneasy about reform. In 1833 they gained control of the Society. Accepting the existing pat-

tern of education, those reformers who favored regulation now staged an attack on certain New York doctors
who had issued medical degrees on the authority of a
diploma mill, the so-called Christian College of the University of Indiana. This case was not simple. Among the
guilty doctors was a prominent homeopath, one of a
group who were leading the fight against the degree
privileges of the College of Physicians and Surgeons, asking instead that all authority to practice derive from
examinations by the medical societies.[42] From this point of
view, the Christian College diplomas were certificates to
those students who had completed private medical studies
under him, and were no more important than he thought
any diploma should be.[43]

The nature of cleavage within the medical community
was shifting again. In 1835 the Society elected a new slate
of "reform" officers, who this time included some homeopaths. This group proceeded to carry out the homeopathic
aim of strict regulation by the society, despite the fact
that they had no statutory authority. They made an elaborate show of staging long, rigorous examinations of certain candidates, apparently in the hope that this would
establish a precedent.[44] Their control of the society,
threatening the political strength and even the claim to
intellectual respectability of the regular practitioners,
aroused the regulars to find a drastic solution to the
crisis that had beset the medical community since the
unsettling effects of the 1827 law.

In 1836 an entirely new grouping arose to take over the
offices of the County Society. All the homeopaths and
their allies lost office. Kappa Lambda men took many
posts, but yielded one to Alexander E. Hosack, a son of
David Hosack who had first been elected to society
office in the reform election of 1831. During the next

few years, John W. Francis took a moderate part in Society affairs.

But Society affairs no longer amounted to much. Whether in deliberate abstention or in unconscious recoil from the acrimony of recent years, members now attended meetings in decreasing numbers. Once a year large numbers turned out at elections to make sure that control of the Society remained with the new coalition, but for the rest of the year there was hardly ever a quorum.[45] Making sure that factional controversy could not disturb the new quiet regime, the Society depersonalized the office of president on July 20, 1840, by stipulating that no individual could hold it for two years in succession. Four years later, the legislature ended any obvious motive that physicians might still have had to join the society by repealing all penal features of the practice law. Long before repeal, though, the medical community in New York City had abandoned any attempt at group life. The remains of the old factions could not agree on any positive program in the early 1840's; they could only neutralize leadership, putting the corporate indentity of the profession into the hands of a caretaking administration.

Some members of the County Society proposed that it surrender its state charter and revert to the condition of a voluntary association.[46] While nothing came of this proposal, it did contribute to a new movement that emerged about 1840 and led eventually to the organization of the New York Academy of Medicine. The principal impulse came from the latest definition of cleavage in the medical community—that is, from the opposition of regular physicians to homeopaths, in contrast to the earlier educational or ideological forms of controversy. The increasing identification of homeopathy as the main

enemy of regular medicine, combined with the influence
that irregulars exerted over the legislature, made it de-
sirable that any new organization be dissociated from
the quasi-public society that homeopaths had once infil-
trated. Only a private organization would have the clear
power to exclude physicians it did not like. The negative
caretaking regime did not suffice, partly because it left
initiative with the homeopaths, and partly because men
like Stearns had long been committed to positive group
action.

All the difficulties since 1790 underlay the fear of individualism that Francis expressed in 1847-48. He knew
how individual ambition had repeatedly split the medical community. He knew that for years the role of aggressive factional leader had been so available that even a
conservative like David Hosack had been drawn into it.
He knew how all attempts at including the medical
community in one organization had confined rivalries
into a system of pressure that burst the organization
itself.[47] Given all this, and given the fact that regular
physicians had found in homeopaths an out-group against
whom they could project some of their intraprofessional
weaknesses,[48] Francis only followed necessity when he
called on doctors to rise above their individual differences.
He was repeating Romayne's old call to liberality, but
with a new seriousness and urgency.

This series of crises in the efforts to work out an over-
all organization for the medical community provides some
explanation of why a spokesman should warn against
intellectual as well as practical individualism. At the
same time, new, small organizations were developing
considerably below the whole-group level. Such organizations were formal equivalents of the "factions" that
medical publicists decried, and often had closer ties to

intellectual effort than did the County Society. Some were student groups, like the Medico-Chirurgical Society of the University of the State of New York, organized in 1807.[49] Like many student clubs, nonmedical as well as medical, this one served ostensibly as a gathering place where the members of a particular student cohort could discuss professional topics and practice professional articulateness. Sometimes a voluntary medical society developed among a younger group of physicians already in practice (as with the Physical Society of 1805), or more particularly among a group of young physicians working together in the same hospital (as with the Medical and Surgical Society, organized in 1839). Often such a society did not last long; the Medico-Chirurgical Society survived only to 1813.

With variation, though, each of these organizations tended to follow a set pattern of development. It began as a small group of aspiring medical men. Because it was weak, it had to seek the patronage of others, perhaps a professor at the school where the members studied, perhaps some older physicians with whom they had good personal relations. As it kept in operation year after year, it lost most traces of its institutional origin. Only by the 1850's did some of the newer such societies become specialized as actual alumni organizations. As the school or hospital base receded, the typical society became more and more a social organization whose members knew each other well enough to share professional experiences and gossip, well enough that they would seek each other out for consultation. Such a society tended to a membership small enough to permit personal contact, yet large enough that fluctuation of individual attendance and interest would not undermine the continued life of the group.[50]

These considerations of size became explicit with the Medical and Surgical Society, organized in the 1830's. It began as a small gathering of physicians of the New York Dispensary. Their meetings lapsed in 1835. Some members then reorganized it in 1836, planning to increase the membership to twenty or thirty, and taking the precaution to ask some older and more influential physicians to join.[51] Now the society survived. It had attained the convenient scale to which such groups tended. It was also the approximate size of the older, unofficial Medical Society of the State of New York that preceded the County Society. Outside the city, some of the chartered county societies preserved this small scale, and with it a solidarity that the New York County Society lacked.[52] From the beginning of the County Society, its efforts to restrict membership never kept it from far outstripping the smaller pattern. Instead, the fraternity or small private society continued what earlier or elsewhere was the pattern for a whole medical community.

In several concrete ways the problems of society organization affected the attitudes of physicians toward medical knowledge. This was less a problem of research in any original sense than of whether doctors would keep up with their study of prior knowledge, with their reading about new developments, and with each other's current experience on cases. For one thing, how would the community make published knowledge available? Would wealthy individuals, small private groups, or large public groups maintain the necessary libraries? During the decade before 1805, everyone involved seemed to assume that the established medical institutions might legitimately operate a library. On the recommendation of the Columbia Medical Faculty, the New York Hospital began a library in 1791; and the Medical

Society began a collection at about the same time. For some reason, though, the Society found keeping its library inexpedient. In 1805, the Society transferred its holdings to the library of the New York Hospital, stipulating that any then members of the Society could have access to the combined library, and that any member's son who became a regular practitioner in New York could also have access.[53]

Over the following generations, the Hospital maintained regulations that at least nominally limited use of the library to physicians of the Hospital and their pupils. Whatever the Medical Society intended consciously, its decision meant that it yielded only its legal identity to the succeeding County Society, reserving its property to another organization representative of the older medical community. But since the property in question was books, this separation of functions meant giving legal activity to the larger community while reserving cognitive or intellectual matters to a smaller, unofficial group. The official County Society did not begin even a meager collection until some time after 1824, and its example stood in contrast to what happened in Columbia County. In this country area, the whole body of respectable practitioners was small. This body became a county society under the 1806 law, ignoring most pressures toward inclusiveness; it began building up a library years before the larger New York County Society began a collection.[54] Even the New York Academy of Medicine, during its early years, could find no real way to implement urgings from its leaders that it maintain a library; not until the 1860's did it become strong enough to move in this positive direction.[55]

The small group also functioned more easily in the role of adviser to the community. As late as the yellow fever epidemic of 1798, the unofficial Medical Society issued a printed report in response to inquiries from the mayor.[56] The Society had, however, already clashed with the College of Physicians over interpreting the epidemic of 1795. This horizontal and social cleavage within the profession cut across the supposedly intellectual disagreement over contagion. Anticontagionists, deriving their ideas from Benjamin Rush, insisted that yellow fever spread from foul conditions in the environment, not by person to person transmission; they urged strict sanitary control but denied the value of quarantines, which disrupted commerce. Contagionists, led in New York by Samuel Bard and David Hosack, defended the traditional precautions. Perhaps because ordinary people feared interference with daily life more than interference with commerce, perhaps because they warmed to a theory that sanctioned an emotional response to disease, the majority in the city seemed to side with the contagionists, while most of the commercial classes and most of the doctors themselves sided with the anticontagionists. In the bitterness of controversy, men paid less attention to a precise third theory that Hosack finally stated, in which he held that the disease, though contagious, was transmitted through the medium of unhealthy conditions in the atmosphere. This interpretation approached the later mosquito explanation as closely as observations and knowledge permitted.

In the epidemics of the 1820's and 1830's, the County Society sometimes conducted discussions and prepared public reports,[57] but in major instances it failed to reconcile the differences among physicians.[58] Such a split developed during the cholera epidemic of 1832, even though most physicians agreed that that disease was contagious. Stearns, the relatively recent migrant to the city, made an early diagnosis of the appearance of Asiatic cholera. According to his account, the mayor and the bulk of the profession refused to accept his diagnosis until the disease had grown into an obvious disaster; one physician called him (in Stearns's words) "a prominent leader . . . injuring our mercantile interests," and charged him with lending his name to "those young men who were not yet known to the public and with having created unnecessary alarm."[59] At least two groups within the medical community tried to profit from the confusion into which cholera threw the profession. Kappa Lambda sought to gain acceptability by publishing two handbooks, one for the public and one for the profession, summarizing the best advice on dealing with the unfamiliar disease. And the homeopaths found that from this period dated their most rapid rise; some of the public were willing to try their answer to the menace, and even some regular physicians, in one homeopath's account, became more friendly during the uncertainty.[60]

During the first part of the nineteenth century, the controversies among regular physicians on such issues as contagionism differed only in degree from the controversies between the regulars and the sectarians or intellectually ambitious quacks. The disease crisis of the early 1830's threatened, however covertly, to bring a spilling over of regular controversy into sectarian schism; the threat may account for the intensity with which regulars united against homeopathy in the middle of the decade. They feared, not just that persons already secessionist would grow in public favor, but also that respectable physicians might decide intellectual issues on an irrational basis, that they would let confusion or social and economic motives become the deciding forces in the intellectual sphere. Men reacted most strongly against that heresy to which they themselves felt vulnerable.

This fear rested on an attitude that most doctors had toward the medical personality: that all doctors quarrel with each other; that the normal relation between any two doctors is animosity, to be overcome only by special arrangements; and that any doctor, as such, will constantly be tempted to choose his ideas and beliefs in such a way as to maximize his chances in economic competition with other doctors. Within all the concern for the solidarity of the whole medical community, within all the impulses to revert to small-scale organization, this attitude lies close to an inward explanation of Francis' intellectual panic in 1847-48.

To some extent the attitude merely reflected popular prejudice, compounding it with perverse self-criticism. Elements of the idea were endemic among doctors. In 1769 a professor of physic warned his students against the dangers of attacks by physicians on other physicians' reputations. He described the subtlety and ease with which the young physician could fall into this vice, and he suggested "Associations of Gentlemen" to provide the "Openess and mutual Confidence becoming FRIENDS, not less zealous for the Honour of their *Profession,* than attentive to the Reputation of each other."[61] Sometimes a physician would argue that doctors' quarrels were not intrinsic to the medical character. David Hosack, who differed strongly from Benjamin Rush on the theory of epidemics, wrote to Rush, "Let us show the world that a difference of opinion upon medical subjects is not incompatible with medical friendships; and in so doing, let us throw the whole odium of the hostility of physicians to each other upon the competition for business and money. Alas! while merchants, mechanics, lawyers, and the clergy live in a friendly intercourse with each other . . . physicians, in all ages and countries, riot upon each other's characters! How shall we resolve this problem in morals?"[62]

But Hosack then was trying to get Rush's support for the amalgamation of the two New York medical schools. Later, at a time when he had been suffering bitterly from party feelings, with which he was himself deeply imbued, he gave his students advice in the older, fully pessimistic vein. He warned against jealousy toward fellow physicians:

Unfortunately in all professions, and indeed in all pursuits, where the mind is actively occupied, there is an excitement and irritability of the nervous system, which while it leads to an ardent desire of excellence and superiority, also creates a feeling of jealousy and envy towards those who may be competitors for the same distinction and public favour. I exempt no profession from those feelings, which, until counteracted by discipline and a strong sense of moral duty, are to a degree inseparable from our nature. Even those whose sacred office it is to inculcate lessons of virtue and religion, with all the control they are enabled to exercise over their own conduct, too frequently betray this characteristic peaceful spirit of the gospel they profess.

He did admit, though, that doctors were peculiarly susceptible to professional jealousy, and he enjoined his students not to refuse professional dealings with colleagues with whom they had personal disagreements: "The physician is a public character; he holds an official station in the community; and therefore, while professing himself a practitioner, cannot be absolved by any private considerations from the discharge of the functions appertaining to that profession."[63] These statements, however much their particulars may have embodied Hosack's anger of 1826, marked the moral peak of his career. In a person of his polemic temper, extending the traditional judgment to other professions provided only the barest decent cover for his admitting that the judgment applied to his own career, that he could preach against sin because he was himself a suitable object of mercy.

Not all physicians equivocated as did Hosack. Even when they moved from the obvious topic of "jealousy" to the sharper fear that physicians would subordinate intellectual integrity to selfishness, they pressed right in to make direct accusations. Cadwallader Colden complained in 1745 that New York physicians had given out little information on their experience with yellow fever; yet he hoped that he, as a physician who had left active practice, might learn something from them: "They may more freely communicate their observations to me than they do to one another for they can not be Jealous of my having any design to supplant them in their trade as they are scandalously so of one another & have thereby render'd themselves & the practise of Physick in this Country contemptible."[64] Although Hosack implied to Rush that there was a valid intellectual difference between contagionism and anticontagionism, those who defended Hosack and his fellow contagionists did not speak so mildly. An admirer of Hosack's teacher Samuel Bard saw the contagionists as a persecuted minority: "I speak here in reference to the controversy as it has been conducted in New-York *only*. Indeed here it has become a *personal* question. Will you side with certain men, or will you join their enemies? The violence on this subject, and the aspect which is given to the controversy, is, no doubt, intentionally excited by designing men. They have taken this road to *importance,* because they cannot succeed in becoming the leaders of a party by more honourable means."[65]

From the 1820's into the 1840's, physicians continued this line of criticism, becoming sometimes more analytical as they ground into cliché the old recommendation that associations be used to curb jealousy. As they now saw this curb, it could act in at least two different ways. An association could criticize and correct the wilder ideas that doctors produced in their irrepressible speculating about disease; and it could undercut any unbased slanders by providing doctors with a continuing way to estimate each other's merits, even after they had left the temporary association of college.[66] This process of evaluation and criticism involved a degree of leveling:

> No man can know precisely the measure of his own ability; his estimate may be, and no doubt sometimes is, correct; but when it is so, it is purely accidental: hence it is, that, for the most part, men of education are divided into two great classes; those who are distrustful of their own powers, and those whom vanity prompts to overrate them. Literary and scientific associations, by bringing various degrees of talent into collision, enable the possessors to correct that false estimate which their timidity or their confidence had formed by showing them in relation; and the emulation of the young aspirant after distinction is so disciplined by the comparisons thus frequently instituted between himself and others, that assurance on the one hand, and an overweening modesty on the other, are made to give place to a well-tempered confidence, which is neither inefficient through fear nor offensive by its arrogance.[67]

The persistently small size of voluntary medical associations made it clear that, without some special ideological effort such as went into the promotion of the New York Academy of Medicine, doctors felt that no large group could provide a sense of solidarity and guarantee against sniping at reputations. Only within the intimate group could intellectual communication move freely. The small private association required, just as it was supposed to produce, unanimity of spirit among its members. The urgency of the requirement became clear when two developments in the New York Medical and Surgical Society demonstrated that even the small society was vulnerable to dissension.

The first of these developments was the removal of homeopaths from membership about 1840. As formed in the 1830's, the society had included only regular physicians, four of whom turned homeopath and dropped out. One of the seceders, Caleb Ticknor, had shortly before his conversion[68] published his own analysis of the attitudes of medical men. He blamed "exclusiveness" and "ultraism" on "avarice," "ambition," and the "passions" generally.

To such an extent are the feelings of hostility carried in the practice of medicine, that one physician will not even use the remedies recommended by one whom he dislikes, when his own reason and conscience, besides his observation and experience, tell, and demonstrate to, him that they are the best adapted in a given case. We could, were it expedient, cite more instances than one, where a writer has warmly praised one plan of treatment for a certain disease, and extolled particular remedies, and when he finds that one whom he dislikes, or whom he considers his mortal enemy, has done the same thing, he has changed his notes of praise into tones of the most bitter denunciation.

.   .   .   .   .

The word of an ambitious professional man—one who is eager for distinction, and desirous of making a noise in the world, without a corresponding wish to advance the interest of science—should be taken, if received at all, at a most liberal discount; he is in the position of a witness in a court of justice, who is interested in the issue of a suit—and who, in the eye of the law, is deemed incapable of speaking the truth.[69]

One of Ticknor's reviewers, after praising him for ex-
posing quackery outside the profession, censured the
passages on ultraism and exclusiveness—not alleging that
they were completely untrue, but that reprehensible physicians were rare and that there was no point in talking
about them in a book intended for the general public.[70]

The Medical and Surgical Society suffered a more
serious split in 1847, the same year that the New York
Academy of Medicine was established. One member,
Horace Green, had developed a technique for treating
inflammations of the larynx by passing a medicated
sponge directly through to the affected area. Around this
technique he built an entire special nose and throat
practice, at a time when doctors still hesitated to accept
specialization. He was not a cautious practitioner, and
he claimed more for his methods than they deserved, but
his opponents chose to call him an outright liar. They
said, incorrectly, that his technique was anatomically
impossible. In 1847 the New York Medical and Surgical
Society forced him to resign, and nearly a third of its
membership quit in protest. Since both of the resulting
factions joined the New York Academy of Medicine,
the Academy itself fell into serious controversy about
Green.[71] The assertive individualist who could disrupt
group life was not just a figure of the past like Nicholas
Romayne. The often observed interplay between competition and the medical intellect could still cause trouble.

If doctors judged the medical personality harshly, some
among them did qualify the judgment by seeing it in the
context of a crude notion of how social relations affected
intellectual life. They saw, for instance, that certain
social groups were apt to furnish clientele for certain
kinds of irregular practitioners.[72] Doctors also sensed differences in the intensity of rivalry from one community

to another, differences that they sometimes related to town size. A medical journalist could agree with a clergyman who thought that doctors were most likely to be social leaders in "smaller towns and settlements."[73] In the rural or near-rural community, the physician had the same sort of local monopoly as the operator of a country store. But as soon as one other physician entered the immediate area, controversy ensued. Caleb Ticknor defined a principle—"If we look for the effect of a restless, ambitious spirit, we shall nowhere see it more manifest than in a densely populated place, where a number of physicians are brought into the same neighborhood"— but he, too, set his definition of dense population low, at those "country towns" where patients' allegiance to particular physicians was passed down from generation to generation.[74]

Above this level, the pattern became less clear. There were some phases, as with New York City in the 1780's or with some of the outlying counties later, in which a relatively simple form of organization seemed to control discord. As communities became cities, however, organization might or might not succeed. The editors of a New York medical magazine printed the following excerpt from a Boston magazine: "A gentleman in a country town, where there are five practitioners of medicine, no two of whom can speak civilly together, desires to know how one hundred can live in Boston without quarreling. Answer. In the first place, every physician in the city is considered a gentleman, till he shows himself to be otherwise. Secondly, each one devotes himself exclusively to his own individual business. Thirdly, they have nothing to quarrel about." On this the New York editors could only comment, "We wish we could say the same of the medical profession in this city. Will the editors of the Boston Medical and Surgical Journal be so good as to inform us what they do with a physician when 'he shows himself to be otherwise' than a gentleman?"[75] Once American communities passed beyond village isolation, physicians began, or perceived that they began, to quarrel among themselves. They soon sought organization that would contain disorder and restore to the physicians as a unit some of the older sense of local influence; yet such organization might fail when the population grew so large that the medical community itself no longer figured as a primary group. Oriented always to some slightly outmoded scale of social order, yet undermined both by new growth and by what physicians themselves thought were the fatalities of medical character, medical organization fell repeatedly off balance and had repeatedly to be re-established.

Doctors like John W. Francis who reacted against cultural individualism were carrying over into cognitive life a response common and recurrent within the economic sphere. Like men in many occupations, they strengthened association among themselves in order to reduce competition. In addition, some doctors consciously sought a leveling conformism as a goal for professional life. This last step arose partly from the very intellectuality of the physicians as a group. Far more than men in most kinds of work, they sought words to describe their position in society. By the early nineteenth century, this seeking produced in American physicians a conception of how certain approaches to knowledge corresponded with certain kinds of social relations. Even if objective conditions did not require cultural uniformity to accompany professional association, the doctors' own ideas suggested that they would have to accept this cultural result in order to obtain their social goal.

Among the pressures that enforced this logic was the actual excess of professional individualism during the first generation of the century. The traditional doctors' quarrels of European and British society had subsided somewhat in colonial America, since physical dispersion and the smaller average size of communities made it possible for a large proportion of doctors to enjoy a monopoly on practice in some locality. This condition ended gradually, of course, and the ending moved rapidly about the beginning of the nineteenth century. At that time a large proportion of physicians, including many who were migrating to populous places from the country, knew or remembered local isolation as a standard even while they sought to work out a life appropriate to the city.

For all its special confusions and complexities, the New York area reflected the style of life in America generally. That life was one version of the provincial life that appeared wherever Europeans had to make their way outside the centers of government and intellect. In southern France and northern England, in the many provincial enclaves of central Europe, the great medical schools and the government-backed medical guilds had less influence than they did in Paris or London or Vienna. Instead, local gentry influence served as a substitute for formal government in allocating standing to practitioners; and local medical families often performed the tasks of recruitment and professional discipline simply by channeling men from the household into practice. This interfusing of family, community, and profession was the first distinct form in which the medical profession was transferred across the Atlantic to America during the eighteenth century, obviating the earlier tendency for clergymen or magistrates to act as physicians. Although in the confusions of colonial life some men set themselves up in practice without any elaborate community ties, the bulk of those who built socially respectable practices came into medicine by the familial or community-based route. For some, communal orientation and training took the form of a term as assistant surgeon to a regiment or as attending physician to a public charity. In the city, membership in a medical family or the enjoyment of public medical office served somewhat the same ends that were served by the isolated monopolies of outlying localities, identifying the significant medical community as a very few individuals who should be accorded public identity and respect. When young doctors chose a place to begin practice, they were often deciding whether to accept the restrictive atmosphere of a city like New York or to move out nearer the actual frontier. Two things are worth noting in this choice. First, though there were in fact many quacks or marginal practitioners working in the city, they may not have been psychologically visible to the man seeking a respectable practice. To him, they were simply part of the urban miscellany, hardly more noticeable than barmaids or street vendors. He noticed more the fact that New York, like any provincial city, was inhospitable to new practitioners. And second, if he moved closer to the frontier, he was seeking his own monopoly quite as much as he did any freedom.

Except for the cities or largest towns, the America of 1800 had conditions suitable for a stable medical life in each community. What America lacked was a set of legitimate opportunities for the individual physician to advance himself and claim special distinction. He could go to the frontier, finding immediate opportunities at the risk of death or rusticity. Or he could seek to impose

himself on the city medical community, appealing to
the long-ignored marginal practitioners to become his
allies. This is what Sir James Jay and Nicholas Romayne
and David Hosack did, each acting the part of raiding
demagogue. Because the main professional institutions
were the family itself, and the medical community itself,
ambition had little outlet except in flight toward the
wilderness or in furnishing leadership to lesser men.
When Samuel Bard and others lifted the community
into established institutional form in the years after
1765, they seemed at first to create the needed scope for
leadership. In fact, though, their little institutions simply
became identified with the older medical community
and with its ingrown familial flavor. The want of individual scope persisted. Repeatedly, men seeking the advancement denied them within the communal profession tried
to expand their chances by using the whole population
of practitioners as a base on which to erect new, more
elaborate, more formal, less personalistic institutions. Just
as often, the narrower population of socially respectable
practitioners worked to cut any new institutions back
within the scope of community life. This byplay went
through several phases, reaching major crises in 1807
and in the years just after 1827. Each level of dispute
sloughed off new factions into the local medical population, creating new bases for quarreling. Thus the attempts
to create formal institutions resulted in intensifying the
excesses of competition, factionalism, and individualism;
and the very fact that no such institutions were yet really
achieved meant that no means existed to restrain individual ambition. In the context of this dilemma, medical
leaders found both institutional coercion and individual
ambition vexatious. Because they wanted to restrain individualism without coercion, they had to find a way

to create some self-regulating "conscience" that would bind the medical community. The most useful form of community conscience was some sort of ideology—in particular, an ideology that became persuasive by joining the social with the intellectual aspects of individual ambition, treating them as if they could not be separated. There was no great logic in fusing these two in order to restrict both, but there was security and comfort to be had in lumping both individualisms together and asking no hard questions about how to distinguish them.

The way out from social disorder led American doctors to a kind of cultural impersonality that minimized the importance of individuality to discovery and insight. To them, ambition was less likely to stimulate research than to corrupt judgment. During the middle years of the nineteenth century, when medical science everywhere seemed to pause in its progress before showing obvious results, the negative aspect of this impersonality seemed to prevail. Francis and others rationalized it, saying that it was necessary to the scientific outlook. And in fact, if impersonality could help to suppress medical wrangling for a time, then a new generation of physicians might develop, freed from the worst fear that originality endangered professional life. The value of this respite from individualism depended on a balancing of results. Which did it do more, strengthen scientific virtue or encourage American mediocrity?

Branding Iron and Retrospect

LAWYERS IN THE CUMBERLAND RIVER COUNTRY

At one point in the records of the circuit court of Sumner County, Tennessee, among many routine entries for the February Term of 1840, there occurs the minute of a trial for assault and battery. In form, the entry differs little from the many others for the same offense, except in its brevity and conclusiveness: the defendant pleads guilty, he is fined five dollars and costs, and that ends the matter.[1] The result is not appealed. What makes the entry peculiar is the identity of the defendant: Josephus C. Guild, who was an active, increasingly successful member of the bar of Sumner County.

The conviction did not interrupt Guild's career. He continued to practice busily not only in the courts meeting in Gallatin (the county seat of Sumner, about forty miles up the Cumberland River valley from Nashville) but also in those of several other upriver towns of Middle Tennessee. He sometimes went down to Nashville to take cases into the Supreme Court. He was elected to the chancery bench in 1860. After the Civil War he moved to Nashville, practiced there, and got elected to the city bench in 1870.[2]

Guild also wrote his memoirs of the Tennessee bar,

memoirs that demonstrated the compatibility between his assault conviction and his continuing career. When he went down from Sumner County to Nashville in 1821 to study law, he went to the courthouse to find a lawyer who conformed to his notions of a great man.

I was a stranger, a "looker-on in Venice." Then for the first time I saw Col. Ephraim H. Foster. He was arguing a case in the County Court, that then had civil and criminal jurisdiction. Col. Robert Weakley, as I afterwards learned, was the presiding justice. Col. Foster and the old Judge got at loggerheads; high words ensued, and each being game-chickens of the most approved blood, a fight ensued. Foster threw a book at the Judge, who left the bench and drew his arms, and prepared to give battle to his antagonist. Foster quickly drew his, and a bloody rencounter would have ensued had not the numerous friends of each interfered and put a stop to the difficulty.[3]

Following Foster to his office, Guild applied to be taken as a student. Accepted, he discovered something he thought odd: that, in the partnership of Brown & Foster, the fiery Foster was the diligent member who prepared the office work and argued cases in lower courts, while the dour William L. Brown not only prepared briefs but argued the really important cases in court. Guild studied in their office for eighteen months, then took his license and returned to Sumner County to open an office.

Once in practice, he did not sit in his Gallatin office waiting for clients; he rode the judicial circuit with all the other lawyers. As he recalled the circuit in later years, it had been the characteristic feature of legal practice in the years before the war. The system required each judge to hold court successively in each county over a large district. He would try cases for a week or so in one county seat, then ride in a body with the attorneys of the court to the next county seat. Traveling together, rooming in

the same inns, drinking together, the lawyers, attorney
general, and judge all came to know each other intimately.
Since they were one big family of high-spirited gentlemen,
they were not always a happy family; but their disputes
reflected the tone of their intimacy. When a judge proved
to be a tyrant, trying to make life hard for an attorney
whose methods he disliked, the whole bar cooperated in
vengeful tricks on the judge. When tempers shriveled and
a lawyer moved in to thrash one of his fellows, the judge
enforced the amenities by visiting a penalty on the offender;
but both the thrashing and the penalty passed as reasonable features of the system. So it was with Guild's assault
conviction in 1840. In principle, of course, these gentlemen worked out their disputes through gentler, more
orderly means: they carried pistols, they were ready to
duel, and they did duel.[4]

For these men whose own blood flowed fast but thick,
animals were important. Each man brought his own horse,
perhaps a horse for a body servant, perhaps another yet
for show or for racing. Guild himself became one of those
lawyers who made of the circuit a racing club. And when
it came to legal business, animals could be as important
as money. Cash was scarce, so that lawyers had to take
fees in cattle. To avoid wear on these "fees" and keep
them in good marketable condition, the members of the
bar joined together to hire a herdsman to keep them
together in one place until their professional owners returned. As Guild described it, a lawyer then needed four
essential pieces of equipment: a good horse, Blackstone,
the Tennessee statutes, and a branding iron for his fees.

Guild was not the only man to describe thus the early
bar. John Catron, whom Jackson appointed to the United
States Supreme Court in 1837, told such stories of the
years between 1815 and 1818.[5] The same image appeared

regularly in accounts of the bar of the old Southwest or
West, forming a clear contrast to the stolidity of such
areas as rural New York, where a circuit judge could
ride dignified and alone from town to town.[6] For the
whole period from the late eighteenth century through
the middle of the nineteenth, the circuit bar seems to
provide the type or image of frontier legal practice. Its
essential features are personalism, organicism, and con-
creteness. Judges did not deal with lawyers as mere officers
of the court who appeared when court opened, presented
their briefs, then hastened back to offices to continue
serious work. They dealt rather with men who were in
literal attendance upon the court, who received clients
in the courtroom or within sight of it, who prepared
briefs (if any) and arguments while lingering so close to
the proceedings that they could hear anything startling
that developed. Both clients and students came to lawyers
because they had seen them act the part of strong personalities in public quarrels or in the somewhat formalized
disputes of court procedure, especially in criminal trials.
Clients sensed in the emotional intensity of life at the bar
a guarantee that the legal profession could never be completely removed from the feelings of ordinary men—even
though that very intensity bound the bar into a closed,
interresponsive unit. Barter in fees, adventurous play with
horseflesh—these stood for the live, tangible unity that
was the bar itself. One trait that this bar lacked, as against
a simple image of an older communal life, was any sense
of local stability. The important community was that of
the professional group itself, which depended on the personal contact of members who moved together against
the background of a series of localities that provided
merely the stuff with which lawyers worked. Where local-

ity was important, it derived from the fact that the court was itself an organization meeting in one particular place at one time, and functioning in terms of the scenes that it produced at such a time; the court was a group of players that went to the people, not an institution of record in which people found rights rendered abstractly permanent.

In time, some lawyers felt unhappy about this picture, even as an image of their past. Joshua W. Caldwell chided Guild for inaccuracy and spluttered at the widespread "disposition to exaggerate the crudeness and roughness of conditions under which the law was then administered." He insisted, "As a rule the lawyers were men of intelligence and education, and not without refinement." But even he described the circuit bar as persisting "down to the present generation"—and he wrote in 1898.[7] This chronological judgment—that the old-time circuit bar was the prevailing pattern through the whole antebellum period, and that lawyers were not forced to accept a newer, commercial, impersonal kind of practice until after the war—jars against insistence on the "refinement" of earlier lawyers. Obviously lawyers were not all of a kind, obviously some were more of the Guild type and others more of the Caldwell type; but this distinction Guild himself recognized in describing the office of Brown & Foster, where he studied, and this recognition did not interfere with his major point. Obviously, too, the kind of lawyer Caldwell chose to remember turned up more often in the larger towns and became the prevailing type as the years went on. But the leeway that such inferences leave is wide: in the development of the Old Southwest, the forty or fifty years before the Civil War were a period of rapid change. Not to pin down more precisely in time the shifts in social tone within the single most important profession of the area would be to admit defeat in attempts at precision.

The precise answer is that Guild was wrong. Records of who practiced where, when, and how much show that the circuit bar operated in the full manner he described only in the first generation of the state's political life. That kind of bar was decaying rapidly when he began to taste its flavor. Tennesseans were by 1820 already moving toward a more complex, less personal, less agrarian style of practical life. In the largest sense, Guild spoke as one of the many people who felt alienated by this change. In detail, though, the reasons for Guild's erroneous view belonged less to popular ideology than to the pressures and opportunities of his own career. The part that he played in legal business showed, from decade to decade, how his views managed to persist within a context that denied them. By devising expedients, even obsolescence hung on for a time.

One can measure the possibility that the circuit life really existed at any particular time by taking the minutes of county courts for those years (or the minutes or appearance dockets of circuit courts that met in the respective counties after the establishment of circuit courts in 1809), by tallying the recorded appearances of each attorney, and by thus comparing the groups of men who practiced at the bars of counties that adjoined or were on the same circuit. Substantial overlap for any year is presumptive evidence that the social system of the circuit bar may have been real at that moment; lack of overlap is pretty good proof that the system was not then real, and it suggests that some other structural features may have characterized the bar for those years.

For a check on the views of men like Guild, the most

useful counties to investigate are Sumner County (Guild's home and base of operations), Davidson County (which was on the same judicial circuit with Sumner from 1806 to 1809 and after 1835), and Smith County (the next county farther upriver from Sumner, which was set off from Sumner in 1799, and which with several other counties was on the so-called "mountain" circuit with Sumner from 1809 to 1835). The county seats of these counties were Gallatin, Nashville, and Carthage, respectively.[8]

At the beginning, as shown by 1790 records, the inter-county bar was real. Ten years later it still showed some life, but the divergence between bars of related counties was becoming at least as real as the overlap. For 1790 terms in Davidson and Sumner counties, the following patterns occur (with numbers of appearances counted only for private attorneys, not public prosecutors):

Davidson County[9]	*Sumner County*[10]
Josiah Love: 56	J. Love: 7
Howel Tatum: 25	Overton: 3
Andrew Jackson: 21	A. Jackson: 3
James Cole Mountflorence: 17	H. Tatum: 2
John Overton: 12	J. A. Sitgreaves: appears for licensing only
J. A. Sitgreaves: 2	J. C. Mountflorence: appears for licensing only
William Rowan: state attorney	Wm. Roan: state solicitor
	H. Lacy: county solicitor

In 1790, the bars of the two counties were virtually identical. In 1800 this identity was seriously diluted:

Davidson County[11]	*Sumner County*[12]
Bennett Searcy: 6	Samuel Donelson: 21
Seth Lewis: 5	John C. Hamilton: 12
Isham Allen Parker: 4	George Smith: 8

Thos. Stuart: 3
Samuel Donelson: 2
John C. Hamilton: 2
Isaac McNutt: 2
James Dougherty: 2
Herndon & Warton: 1
Wm. P. Anderson: 1
McNutt and Donelson: 1
Wharton & Dougherty: 1
Herndon & Stuart: 1
Herndon: 1
Jessie Wharton: 1

Benjamin Seawell: 7
Thomas Stuart: 3
Thomas Stuart & J. C. Hamilton: 2
Isaac McNutt: 1
James Dohertie: 1
S. Donelson & Geo Smith: 1
Joseph Herndon & Thos. Stuart: 1
John Dickinson: appears for licensing only
Lemuel Henry: appears for licensing only
John B. Johnson: appears for licensing only
Nicholas Perkins: appears for licensing only

Most of the names are the same on the two lists; but the three leaders of the Davidson bar (leaders at least in the sense of the number of cases recorded by their names) do not appear on the Sumner list, while the leaders of the Sumner bar either do not appear on the Davidson list or appear with only minor frequency.

But compare the following pattern in the new Smith County of attorneys practicing at about the same time (1800): Seawell: 4, and also as public prosecutor; Hamilton: 3; N. Perkins: 1; George Smith: 1.[13] Smith County, while attached to the same judicial district as both Davidson and Sumner, was more closely associated with Sumner in both geography and immediate administrative history. This group of four lawyers is largely a selection out of the secondary ranks of the Sumner bar. Physical nearness and shared experience still led lawyers to build patterns

of practice across county lines. Intercounty practice did
have much the concrete, blooded quality that later memoirs reported. It was a young Sumner County lawyer who
in 1801 inserted this notice in a Davidson County paper:

> Those indebted for the last season of Medley,
> are requested to pay either Cash or Produce,
> Cotton or Pork, to Messrs. Tait and Stothart,
> at their former Store in Nashville, and their
> receipt shall be admitted by
> ### R. D. BARRY[14]

The little set of early data on Smith County, when
compared with the 1790 figures on Davidson County,
brings out another structural feature of the early bars,
although one that had no direct bearing on the problem
of the traveling circuit bar. In the initial years of any
bar, lawyers were so few that those available had a
monopoly of practice. It was difficult to find enough lawyers to take both sides of every case, and public prosecutors were allowed to take private causes at the same
term in which they did public business. The leading
attorney or partnership of the bar handled more than a
third of the cases, and the top two attorneys far more
than half. In a professional situation where there had to
be at least two practitioners to handle business in any
meaningful way at all, this was a high degree of concentration. To be sure, the scarcity-concentration patterns
were much stronger for Davidson and Sumner counties
in the 1780's, when those counties first had working bars,
than they were a little later, but the measurable degree of
concentration persisted well after strict monopoly had
ended. Even while new individuals were constantly gaining admission to the bar, the domination of practice by
one or a few leaders persisted.

As might be predicted from comparison with, say, the

grocery business in the early nineteenth century, concentration was more marked in the smaller towns. Samuel Donelson and John C. Hamilton had between them over 60 per cent of the practice of Sumner County in 1800, while Bennett Searcy and Seth Lewis had only a third that of Davidson County. In the district court for the Mero District, which included all of the Cumberland River country, the pattern of appearances for the May Term of 1800 fell rather between the Sumner and Davidson degrees of concentration:

Mero District[15]

Seth Lewis: 16	James Dohertee: 1
Bennet Searcy: 14	J. C. Hamilton: 1, and also
Howel Tatum: 14	district attorney
Samuel Donelson: 3	Benj. Seawell: 1
G. W. Campbell: 3	Herndon: 1
John Overton: 3	George Smith and Thos.
Jenkin Whiteside: 2	Stuart: 1
W. P. Anderson: 2	John Dickinson: appears
Thos. Stuart: 2	for licensing only

Then between 1800 and 1810 the difference between the amounts of legal practice in Davidson and in Sumner exploded, as shown in the figures for 1810:

Davidson County[16]	*Sumner County*[17]
John Dickinson: 97	John H. Bowen: 11
Felix Grundy: 68	Thomas Stuart: 7
O. B. Hayes: 39	H. L. Douglass: 4
John E. Beck: 34	B. H. Henderson: 3
Thomas Stuart: 34	R. D. Barry: 3
Bennett Searcy: 33	Felix Grundy: 2
William Smith: 20	John C. Hamilton: 1
Jesse Wharton: 17	Jenkin Whiteside: 1

Robert Searcy: 13   Jesse Wharton: 1
Jenkin Whiteside: 11   Grundy & Barry: 1
Thomas Claiborne: 11
(and seven other attorneys
   with three or fewer appearances each)

Despite the shift in scale, some of the structural relations
between the two bars persisted. Although open to many
practitioners, and giving to them varying amounts of
business, the larger of the two bars showed a marked
pattern of leadership, reflecting especially the fact that
in the many debt-collection cases of that year John Dickinson acted as the chosen attorney for the plaintiff, while
Felix Grundy acted often for the defendant. The smaller
bar showed almost as high a concentration of practice as
in earlier years, with the leading attorney taking nearly
a third of the cases and the two leading together taking
over half. And as before, the overlap of individuals between the two bars hardly fitted any picture of a vigorous
traveling bar—which is hardly surprising, since by 1810
Davidson and Sumner counties had been separated, with
Sumner put on the mountain circuit. Although most of
the very active attorneys in Sumner County did not appear on the Davidson list at all, the positions of Thomas
Stuart and several of those who were less active in Sumner suggest that attorneys from the larger place could
take cases in the smaller place simply because they were
from the big town: they had greater prestige, and they
had more of the centralized business connections that
might be relevant to certain cases.

   Circuit courts that moved from county to county
within a defined area were actually new in 1810, having
been pushed through the legislature in 1809 by Thomas

Hart Benton, then a young Nashville lawyer. Before that —during the years when intercounty practice had been most real—the principal courts had been the county courts, which had no conclusive jurisdiction, and the district courts, which heard appeals at some fixed point within each district. The ostensible reasons for this creating of actual, formal circuits were those presented by Benton when he signed his newspaper articles "Sir John Oldcastle" in 1808: that the district courts were not so constituted that they could handle all their business, and that it was oppressive to plain men to make them take their lawsuits from their own counties to some other distant county where the district court met.[18]

The real reasons for the change may have had less to do with these proper arguments than with the differences that working lawyers saw between the two systems. John Overton, the Nashville judge and compiler of the first important series of Tennessee legal reports, conducted a running correspondence during these years with certain lawyers in East Tennessee. One was Thomas Emmerson of Knoxville, a Federalist who handled much of the printing and publication of the reports. Emmerson complained that under the new system the court above the circuit courts had little dignity, implying that it could regain stature only if the system were revised to give stability, adequate pay, and light court loads to judges. Complaining about the physical burden and about the low quality of juries under the circuit system, he rode circuit over a wide area of East Tennessee until 1816, when he gave up and went into banking.[19] Another of Overton's correspondents came to feel that the new system favored lawyers' practices over judicial respectability. While he wrote hesitantly in the fall of 1810—"I yesterday returned from Claiborne which clos'd my Circuit in the Circuit Courts for the second round of the first Circuit, there is no great deal of business here tho' what there is I have had a reasonable share. I have collected but little yet but have made considerably more in Notes Horses promises &c. than a years salary of a Tennessee Judge"—he made a blunt judgment the following spring: "I have been much engag'd in my professional pursuits for this year past, and have succeeded quite as well as I had any reason to expect. I think I make nearly or quite twice as much as my salary as a Judge amounted to. I find the Circuit system advantageous to Lawyers generally and if I consulted my own interest only I think I should be in favour of the system, but as things are going on under it I do believe if continued as it is it will be the greatest curse that ever infested this state[.]"[20]

The circuit system, coming out of the western parts of the state at a time when that area was beginning to outgrow the earlier, spontaneous intercounty bar, asserted the interests of lawyers against judicial centralization— and probably against the concentration of legal business in the hands of a few dominant lawyers. Later, lawyers sometimes "remembered" that they had had to go on circuit because business was too scarce in any one place. This was almost true, but not quite. Except in very small or very new counties, a fair amount of business was available in any one place; but the control that a few lawyers had over most of this business meant that the marginal and even the middle-level practitioner had to scour widely to get enough for himself. The new system did not actually work against the top-ranking lawyers; rather, it worked to preserve or find opportunities for those of lesser rank, and in a way that dissipated the sharpness of competition between practitioners.[21]

Overton's correspondence also shows how the subject

matter of legal practice retained a personal, slow-moving quality, even as the potentiality of something smoother, more commercial, and more fluid was beginning to develop. The smoother potential lay in debt collections, which were to be the superficially dominant form of legal business a generation later. By 1810 or earlier, some lawyers had already formed connections with Philadelphia banks, from which they received notes for collection in Tennessee. And by then the 5 per cent commission on collections was established as standard in local practice.[22] But Thomas Emmerson seemed almost unhappy that commercial problems were not what gave him an argument for the importance of judges:

> Whether our infant State of Society has the tendency you ascribe to it of simplifying our legal Code or of rendering the duty of a Judge less arduous, appears to me very questionable; for altho' it be true that the subjects of dispute are less numerous than in a Wealthy and populous Society, and tho' many intricate branches of the Law are applicable only to such Commercial Transactions as can never occur among us, are unnecessary to be attended to here—yet it is to be considered that our Laws respecting real property are to say the least not less intricate than those of any other state—in addition to this the loose and unskilfull manner in which our Citizens & Legislatures are too apt to transact their business, is continually giving rise to new questions many of which present great and real difficulties.[23]

This may be translated, of course, as a conflict between "Federalist" and "frontier" ideas of what the bar should be. It may also, and without bias as to historical labels, be read as a conflict between those men who wanted the legal profession to have a formal, hierarchic character and those men who sought to minimize formality in favor of a more personal way of doing business. What

Josephus C. Guild later recalled as a chronological shift in the style of professional life was already a byplay between conflicting styles, a byplay in which hierarchic ways met strong resistance from the personalistic style that Guild remembered favorably.

But the bar, while already changing, changed at different rates in different jurisdictions. Take the matter of size. By 1810 the Davidson County bar, working in the "big city," Nashville, had shifted from a scarcity of talent to a plethora, leaving the Sumner County bar, by contrast, a compact group. The same pattern continued over the whole next generation, as is shown by several different groups of data for 1840. Again, the number of times a lawyer appeared as attorney furnishes a measure of his activity.

Davidson County Circuit Court[24]

Appearances for the Plaintiff

Ewings: 72
C[– – –]? & Fletcher: 34
Foster & Fogg: 32
Washington & Hay: 13
Lindsley: 9
Grundy & Southall: 8
Cook: 7
Perkins: 7
Trimble: 6
Meigs and Brown: 6
R. C. Foster, 3d: 5

(and nine other attorneys with fewer than five appearances each)

Appearances for the defendant

Grundy and Southall: 40
Ewings: 35
C[– –]? & Fletcher: 26
Hollingsworth: 20
Cook: 9
Lindsley: 7
Garland: 6
Williams: 5

(and 13 other attorneys with fewer than five appearances each)

Sumner Circuit Court[25]	Sumner Chancery Rule Docket[26]	Sumner Chancery Enrolling Docket[27]
J. J. White: 13	Guild: 32	Guild: 17
Jo. C. Guild: 7	White: 13	Trousdale: 7
Blackmore: 7	Trousdale: 9	White: 3
Trousdale: 6	Baldridge: 6	H. S. Kemble: 2
Trousdale & Guild: 1	Cook: 3	F. B. Fogg: 1
Patterson: 1	Kemble: 3	Burton: 1
Guild & Blackmore: 1	Cook & Guild: 2	Cook: 1
James J. Bracken: 1	Allen: 2	Baskerville: 1
Tremble: 1	Cook & Boyd: 1	
	Baskerville: 1	
	Burton: 1	

While the variations between these Sumner County patterns are enough to enjoin some caution about the usefulness of dockets as exact indexes of professional structure, the patterns do converge on at least one point: in any line of practice, the lawyers of Sumner County were few enough that they might know each other personally. This compactness was less marked in Smith County, which at that time had a relatively large area and equaled Sumner in population both of the county and of the county seat, but did not equal it in density of population, in vocational heterogeneity of the whole county population, or in number of lawyers:[28]

Smith County Circuit Court, Law Docket, April Term 1840[29]

Stokes & McClain: 23	Trousdale: 1
Caruthers: 22	Campbell: 1
Overton: 18	Coggins & McD.: 1
McClain: 16	Patterson: 1
McDonald: 12	Williamson & P.: 1

Brien: 8   Cullom: 1, and also as at-
Ferguson: 4   torney general in crim-
Burton: 2   inal cases
Stokes: 2

After another twenty years, though, Sumner County had
moved noticeably away from compactness, as the following pattern shows:

Sumner Chancery Rule Docket, 1860[30]

Guild, Bennet & Smith	29	Sanders & Stanton	3
Guilds & Smith	17	Sanders	2
Bennet and Smith	4	Stanton	1
Guild	3		—
Bennet	1		6
	—	Solomon & Hubbard	1
	54	Solomon	1
Head & Turner	45	Hubbard	3
Turner	2		—
	—		5
	47	Munday	23
B. F. Allen	7	White	4
G. W. Allen	5	Allen H. & Turner	1
Allen	7	Allen H. Smith & Wilkins	1
G. W. & B. F. Allen	3	Henderson	1
	—	Brien	1
	22	Peyton	1
Winchester & Bate	6	Alexander	1
Winchester	1	Shane	1
Bate	1	Barksdale	1
	—		
	8		

In contrast to this, the Davidson bar had changed little;
its 1860 docket seemed on the surface merely a swollen
version of its 1840 record:

Davidson County Circuit Court, 1860[31]

Appearances for the plaintiff	Appearances for the defendant
Ewing & Cooper: 25	Fosters & McEwen: 57
Vaughn: 20	Brien & Sons: 26
Fosters & McEwen: 20	Wilkin & Wilkin: 23
Demoss: 19	Vaughn: 18
Jno. Reid: 16	Henry M. McEwen: 18
Wilkin & Wilkin: 14	Smiley: 11
Houston & Brown: 11	Ewing & Cooper: 10
N. D. Cross: 11	Meigs: 8
Schon & Merritt: 9	N. D. Cross: 8
Washington: 8	Brien & Cox: 7
Brien & Cox: 8	Schon & Merritt: 7
Brien & Sons: 8	Bradford & East: 6
G. M. Fogg: 7	Demoss: 6
Avis Brown, Jr.: 7	Trimble: 6
Flippin: 6	(and 40 other attorneys with fewer than five appearances each)
Bradford & East: 5	
Baxter & Haywood: 5	
(and 50 other attorneys with fewer than five appearances each)	

The picture of plethora would become even more striking if set up for the Supreme Court, which after 1834 drew into one place in each of the three geographic divisions of the state a representative number of leading lawyers from many counties. During this period, only the rare attorney or firm had more than ten motions docketed at any term of the Supreme Court, and few had more than four or five; the business was much less concentrated than it was in the circuit courts, and the business of the court was brought in by scores of lawyers from many counties, all together forming a large, amorphous state bar.

This developing plethora, if it is supposed to indicate an open market of professional talent at the bar, had some flaws. One was the fact that, in this society even more than in a more thoroughly commercial society, many persons did not restrict themselves to legal practice. The "bench and bar" annals of Tennessee for this period are full of gentlemen who married land and settled on it, and of politicians (not just the obvious "statesmen") who moved in and out of practice in an irregular way. In Nashville, many lawyers were young men who moved over into business before they had had time to develop much practice. Others were older men who no longer had to take any cases except important ones, or ones that interested them. Or they were older men whose statement that they took only the cases they chose was a graceful way to cover failing powers.

But the serious flaw was that each bar, after its first ten or twenty years of getting started as a social organization, settled into a certain degree of concentration of business that persisted for decades as a framework within which individual lawyers found places for themselves. The circulation of individuals through the framework, by success and failure, by licensure and death, seemed to have little effect on the patterns. At the Davidson County bar, in any year, one or two top men had far more business than did any other individuals, from two to six secondary leaders had substantial amounts of business; and a small group of tertiary leaders had respectably more business than the broad scattering of lawyers who seemed lucky to get more than one or two court cases per term. The pattern in Sumner County was generally similar, except that there were not enough lawyers to form any kind of tertiary group distinct from the scattering of nominal practitioners. But if pattern is summarized in terms of the number of lawyers whom one must group in order to account for 50 per cent of the business, then the difference becomes more strict. In the case of the Davidson circuit bar, it took about the top five lawyers to account for half the business in any year. In Sumner, on the other hand, the top two lawyers usually had very close to half the business, and the top three usually had far more than half.[32] This difference between two (or three) and five is critical here. In a court system where there must usually be two parties to a case, the lawyer or firm who takes half the business has as near a monopoly as he can get, short of so frightening people with his prowess that no one will appear against his clients. Similarly, if any two lawyers take as much as half the business of a court, they dominate the market for legal talent. It would seem much less reasonable to say that five lawyers "dominate" practice by obtaining half the business.

Explanations for these degrees of concentration can only be sketched from certain hints of evidence. The techniques for concentrating business can be observed at work, both in the statistical record and in less abstract material. Up to about 1820 in Davidson County, and up to nearly 1850 in Sumner, lawyers practiced as individuals, only occasionally forming *ad hoc* partnerships for particular cases. After these dates most of the more successful lawyers practiced in firms, through which they could handle varied business more efficiently, and through which they did in fact increase considerably the degree of concentration. The process can be seen in the Sumner data for 1860, when partnerships were still unstable, having appeared only recently as a dominant feature of the local bar. In the Davidson bar, at that time, individuals from partnerships sometimes took cases on their own; but this did not affect the total picture. For Sumner, a grouping of cases according to the broader partnership alliances of attorneys shows a marked step upward in concentration from the degree that would be implied by treating separately all the appearances of individual lawyers. During these years the Sumner lawyers seem to have found the business at their circuit court increasing in volume past the point where they could rely on the small-scale bar to keep practice comfortable and orderly. They therefore took to partnerships as a device for fitting a larger volume of business into a more comfortable social framework. They could take up the device readily because they had had much opportunity to observe it in the larger nearby bar of Davidson County. This timing may help to account for the lesser degree of concentration at the Davidson bar. To be sure, the volume of business was inevitably much larger in Nashville than in Gallatin, and partnership was probably not a completely efficient device for limiting the number of units operating in the professional market. But Nashville had moved into the partnership stage a generation before Gallatin. The possibilities of the device may have been less clear then, the expectations of local lawyers as to what share of business they should control had certainly had less time to harden into any pattern, and the Nashville bar had in fact moved into its more diffuse pattern of concentration by 1810, well before partnership appeared on the local legal scene.

Partnership was indirectly related to another principal device of concentration: specialization. One early kind of specialization was that between the plaintiff lawyer and the defense lawyer, resulting partly from the fact that the role of defense lawyer held out to the politician great possibilities for attracting attention and favor. If one of two leaders at a bar took this role, the other would almost inevitably concentrate on the plaintiff side. Thus in 1810 Felix Grundy took the defense, not just in the criminal cases for which he was praised in popular accounts, but in a fair proportion of the debt cases brought in Davidson County; John Dickinson appeared as the lawyer for the opposing side. (And it should be noted that, in contrast to Grundy's reputation for never losing but one murder case, he lost many of the debt suits, some of them involving quite respectable amounts.) Grundy was never rigid about appearing only for the defense in civil cases; he appeared often for the plaintiff in 1810, and in 1820 he was one of three lawyers or firms who appeared regularly for a Nashville bank that was pressing debts.

The full implications of debt collection appeared in the wasting away of the old-time circuit bar. As a literal grouping of lawyers traveling with one circuit court, this bar had long since become a fiction. In Sumner and Davidson counties, which were on the same circuit, only an occasional Gallatin lawyer went into Nashville. In the tabulations for Davidson County given above, most of these trips across the county line involved appearances below the frequency at which it seemed feasible to tabulate individual attorneys' names. In 1840, the last of the years of comparison for which circuit court data are available from Smith County, three lawyers from Sumner County entered one or two motions each on the Smith circuit docket; the great bulk of business was done by local men. More exact data on the meaning of intercounty practice emerge from the dockets of cases brought into the Supreme Court from Smith and Sumner counties in 1850 and 1860:

Supreme Court Law Docket, 1850[33]

From Sumner County	From Smith County
Guild: 3	Hart: 3
Munday: 2	J. S. Brien: 3
Moss & Munday: 1	Wm. Cullom: 3
Moss: 1	J. B. Moores: 2
Blackmore & Barry: 1	Guild & Cullom: 1
Barry: 1	Guild: 1
Baldridge & Head: 1	Fite: 1
	J. B. Moores & J. G. Frazier: 1
	Caruthers & Brien: 1

Supreme Court Law Docket, 1860[34]

From Sumner County	From Smith County
Head & Turner: 3	J. B. Moores: 10
Ewing & Cooper: 1	McClain: 5
Bradford & East: 1	Wm. H. DeWitt: 4
Guilds & Smith: 1	A. M. McClain & W. H. DeWitt: 1
	J. C. Guild & J. B. Moores: 1
	Head & Turner: 1
	Brien: 1
	Williams: 1

Lawyers from outside Smith County, including some from Sumner, occasionally did take cases in Carthage. (There is no reason to believe, from the nature of the Supreme Court record, that these Sumner County lawyers entered cases only after appeal from the circuit court to the Supreme Court.) The bulk of the Carthage business was done, though, by men like Moores and McClain, who were local residents. When J. C. Guild went to Carthage, he went as an *ad hoc* partner of one of the local men. Partnership here had a dual function: it gave a man like Guild, who thought in terms of operating across county lines, entree into courts where he might otherwise have got no business. And, in an up-country bar where some operation by lawyers from other towns was probably inevitable, it served to protect the local lawyers' position of leadership by confining the outsiders in a clearly defined role.

It was in this context of an intercounty practice defined within modest limits that the growing specialization in debt collection affected the structure of legal practice. This growth was recorded fairly precisely in the newspaper advertisements, or "cards," that lawyers inserted in Tennessee newspapers over most of this period. Such cards began to appear as early as 1802 and continued to appear even well after the Civil War, though with decreasing frequency as professional advertising acquired the stigma of vulgarity. At first the cards were general in form, asserting that a lawyer had an office in a certain town and would attend the courts of certain counties; these counties formed a convenient territory over which the lawyer could ride, but only occasionally coincided with a judicial circuit. Among the lawyers who inserted such cards were prominent leaders as well as needy beginners.

Then about 1819, while these general cards continued to appear in the papers, a new kind emerged: a lawyer added, to his statement that he would welcome all kinds of business, the specification that he would give special attention to debt collections in his chosen area; or a lawyer, often one who had come originally from Middle Tennessee, announced that he had taken up residence in some place like Natchez and would attend to business (obviously including collections) in that area. Similarly, a Gallatin lawyer might advertise in Philadelphia that he would attend to collections in Tennessee.[35] This mixed pattern of general and collection cards continued into the 1830's, reflecting the process by which previously unspecialized lawyers were being drawn into a nationwide, increasingly impersonal commercial network. From about 1840 on, collection cards predominated, with the first such card appearing in the Carthage press in 1846. While general cards did continue to appear in the Gallatin paper, they disappeared from Nashville papers, leaving only the collection cards. Advertising by lawyers began to decline in Nashville during the 1840's and 1850's,[36] revealing that the more respectable part of the bar no longer operated as a public institution whose members advertised for practice from any farmer or planter who rode into town on a court day and picked up a newspaper. After about 1820 some leading lawyers had found a large part of their practice through business retainers; this, and growing ties of "connection" and recommendation, came to dominate genteel practice, leaving the mechanical reliance on the court system largely to the debt-collecting lawyers. Debt collection was becoming so routine that even collecting lawyers tried to collect first and only take cases to court if it was absolutely necessary later. The process of collection, which in 1810 had been a proper matter for legal quasi-combat between duel-minded lawyers in the courtroom, was by 1850 well on the way to becoming the routine process that specialized firms might remove from the usual sphere of legal practice. In the meantime, debt collection was a way to drum up practice, just as intercounty practice was, and the two ways converged: the particular counties that a lawyer took for his area were the same ones to which he could conveniently travel with overdue notes, not those to which he followed a migrating bar.

It is true that in the very early frontier days of Middle Tennessee the legal profession worked as if it were a corporate body, taking whole local publics as its clients. Individual lawyers may have thought of themselves as proud men of honor, fighting with forensics or with pistols, but they still presented themselves as a small group to a public that had to use these few lawyers for many cases. The courts then operated as a clearing house for all kinds of economic disputes. But this nominally freewheeling profession was actually inflexible and rigid. As a social organization it did its work under the indispensable personal supervision of one man (the judge) and a clerk, and it consisted of a few licensed disputants. The more competent of these few lawyers would not bother attending without some prospect that they could take a good share of the work channeled through the organization. Beginning as early as the stringencies before the War of 1812, the recurrent pressures of "bad times" brought successive waves of debt work into the courts. Such business, which seemed routine in character to all those who were not immediately involved, crowded court schedules to such an extent that there was too little time and too little flexibility of procedure for the more complex, varied work. This bore hard on the traditional land disputes of the area, which like all land disputes tended to drag through the courts quite long enough as it was. It also left little opening for the growing banks, railroads, and commercial firms to operate within the communal court framework. The creative innovations that Tennessee lawyers produced in these years dealt with precisely this area of problems. In 1819 William L. Brown (the dour partner of Ephraim H. Foster) devised a statute of limitations that set a term on all subsequent land disputes; and John Catron made his first great success by arguing through the courts an interpretive doctrine that extended the quietus to retrospective cases.[37] Later, the emergence of debt collection as a legal specialty of only middling prestige reflected a pressure on lawyers to orient themselves to particular clients, including corporations, rather than to a series of local publics that culminated in the larger court of state politics. Without this shift to practice based on advice given outside the courtroom, professional leadership could hardly have kept up with the expansion of population and business. And it was not merely the expansion of business, but expansion against the communal rigidities of an earlier system, that forced the emergence of a new kind of legal profession.

Josephus Guild was right in sensing the tone of the shift in legal practice, but he was wrong in his description of how it worked and when it took place. The true frontier bar hardly lasted, in Davidson County, beyond the brief early period when Jackson and his associates engaged in active practice. In Sumner County, by the time Guild got into practice there, this kind of bar was already decaying. Why, then, his error and romantic view? The best clues come both from the stages of Guild's own career, and from the particular errors he made when he looked at the past. He came from a village in the back part of the Cumberland River country at a time when the centers of that country had been developing a brilliant leadership—sporting, blooded, and sometimes lawyerly. On his way to that society, he studied for a short time in Gallatin, then for a longer period in Nashville. As a raw aspirant entering Nashville, he made the characteristic mistake of assuming that the difference between stolid and sporting temperaments in the members of a law firm (Brown & Foster) would correspond to the allocation of professional tasks between them. Guild then returned to Gallatin, and spent much of the rest of his life trying to preserve the temperament of the sporting lawyer. He raced horses in several counties. He forced such devices as the *ad hoc* partnership that took him into various counties on business. The business that he got in this way could not have amounted to more than a fraction of what he did in his home county, and probably would have been less than what he could have got by turning to Nashville rather than to the mountain counties for supplements to his Sumner County work. Guild continued this pattern up to the time of the Civil War. After the war he moved into the city, where the state, to take care of the large amounts of court business, set up a special Law Court for Nashville alongside the regular circuit court; Guild was elected judge of this court, and was its only judge before it was abolished in 1877.[38] He complained that the war had destroyed the kind of bar he had known earlier, bringing instead a commercial, corporate system that forced him to move into the city. Actually, though, the bar he recalled had never flourished during his working years. If the war had anything to do with this outcome, it simply helped make obsolete the sporting life that a once-young Guild had persisted in trying to weld to his professional career.

If the restrospective error resulted from the mere compulsions of one man, they would serve as a needed warning, but little more. The point is that these were not "mere" compulsions; they related to some of the important functions of a profession in a developing society. A profession helps to channel social mobility, both on upward lines toward status and on centripetal lines toward

town or metropolitan life. The individuals involved cannot see at the beginning where they are going. Simply
because they are not there yet, they must operate on a
more or less simplified image of their destination. Guild,
in his romanticizing, only exaggerated a simplification
that many of his fellows shared. As he eventually, if im-
perfectly, recognized, he did not operate at the center of
the important, coming kind of legal practice of his day.
His image of the circuit bar thus reassured him that he
was working within what continued to be an important
and wide-ranging social system, just as it had earlier
furnished a reassuringly concrete goal toward which to
work. The war, finally, served as the scapegoat on which
he could unload the unrealisms that had developed around
the circuit image. The successful small-town lawyer found
mobility—up to a point. Beyond that point, he needed
something to rescue his sense of career from encroaching
urban and commercial growth. At best, the something
might salvage the sense of career in a way that tied together the various efforts and images, the various transi-
tions of scene or social level, that had marked a whole
professional life. This was the erring function of retrospect.

Permanency in the New England Clergy

THE GENERAL PROBLEM AND THE NEW HAMPSHIRE CASE

Some problems in the history of the "professions" bear on only one or a few of these occupations; they thus differentiate between the callings that common usage lumps together under one label. For instance, one problem that worried American clergymen in the nineteenth century bore little on the situation of lawyers and physicians. Quietly in the 1790's, then with anxious repetition after 1820, ministers who had enjoyed status and long tenure in their communities complained at the imminent or actual passing of this old order. By the 1830's some among them —the New England Congregationalists—had successfully institutionalized this complaint into a measurable ideal. The ministry, they said, had lost its "permanency"; and they scrambled through committees and exhortations and resolutions after some way of regaining that status.

Before the turn of the century, a man was ordained early in life to the pastorate of a particular local church, receiving thereby the right, sometimes legal and always moral, to stay there as pastor until he died. He, in turn, was obliged to stay there unless the church agreed to let him go and a council of churches gave him a formal dismission. As was true in many aspects of New England church life, contract sufficed to create a relationship, but the relation then had sacred, organic status. Yet by 1840 this organic status had degenerated into a merely quantitative permanency that few ministers any longer achieved. Churches and ministers made contracts limited to five years or one year, or made contracts dissolvable by notice from either party. The minister felt that he was no better off than a Methodist circuit rider.

Neither the lawyer nor the physician faced the same problem. Each worked in a particular locality, and with certain exceptions was as much implicated in the life of the community as any minister. (The exceptions had mainly to do with the role in legal practice of circuit courts and higher courts of appeal.) The local character of these professions was never questioned in a way hostile to the practitioners, hardly questioned at all except through the rise of nonlocal institutions that gave individuals new scope for practice. But this lack of institutional scope was precisely the point. The physician treated natural individuals. The lawyer, unless he became a judge or a public attorney, represented natural individuals or corporate persons. Not until the rise of the engineering profession after 1816 were there many professionals who as types were devoted to serving organized groups. It was the minister who typically worked within and for such a group, yet who had also a direct, authoritative, and often intimate influence on individuals. Depending on how full a roster of professionals a citizen found in his community, he could change lawyers or physicians without incurring anything worse than a little trouble and the risk of offending a particular practitioner. He could not change ministers without committing heresy, schism, or a major change in residence. The secular professions lacked authority and monopoly over their clients. Even if a lawyer or physician practiced for long in one place, he presented no threat of accumulating power. The minister did. The general public, whatever resentments it might hold against the law and medicine, could hardly see local stability as an element touching off that resentment. They could and did see local connection as an element in the minister's strength.

The ministry in the eighteenth century was an office-holding profession, more akin to the European military than to any other American occupation. The law and medicine, on the other hand, were fee-for-service professions, dependent on something resembling market transactions, implicated in a social order more fluid, rationalistic, and openly calculating than anything the ministry was supposed to know. While the accusation of monopoly might be made against attorneys or physicians, they did not enjoy the same problems of office and tenure as did clergymen. The difference between the two kinds of profession was exemplified in different uses of the concept of licensing. Governments or authorized professional associations often gave licenses to practice law or physic; the professions accepted such licensing in the eighteenth century, and it was innovation when some men began to demand that licensing be supplanted by laissez faire. The churches, however, or at least congregational churches, shied away from licensing, which appeared as an innovation in the eighteenth century when the churches needed to exercise some control both over itinerant preachers and over their own domestic missionaries who could not always be distinguished from itinerants. Even so, "license" was an improper word, and sensitive clergymen preferred to speak of "approbation."[1]

To the extent that the minister competed with the lawyer or the physician, he depended on the community as a base of operations. Through the colonial period, an occasional minister practiced medicine on the side, thus supplementing his income or asserting his comprehension of the world. For him to take this extra role, he had to rely on people's confidence in him as a figure in the neighborhood; he had also to rely on people's indifference to specialization. Both of these requirements were best met by a ministerial life embedded in the community. Similar considerations applied to the law. For church members, until the end of the eighteenth century, ecclesiastical courts in which the minister's views had influence channeled much of any ordinary propensity to litigate.[2] Since the ultimate sanction of these courts was excommunication, their authority depended on the vigor and indispensability of the local religious community. Since the minister had technical authority within such a court only through his voice as another church member, his broader influence in the court depended on the weight people accorded to his knowledge of them and their affairs. Community was necessary on both levels: to the court, and to the minister's position in the court. If community ties broke, the minister might still choose to perform legal or medical tasks, but he might find that such performance required him to change from "being a pastor" to "being a doctor."

In the earlier years, churches and ministers alike acted on the belief that they were bound in a relation that should last out and even express the life cycle of any man who became the head of a church. Often a pastor did become too feeble or befuddled to preach, or too cantankerous to handle ordinary dealings with his people. When his incapacity became too great, the church and town then called another man to be colleague pastor, relieving the old man of duties but not removing his salary and perquisites. At worst, he might give up some of his salary to help pay the younger man.[3] The law did require a town to maintain some kind of minister, and it did give a settled minister a claim to continuing support. But it did not require a town to support a second minister, and it did not really forbid a town to use extralegal or even sharp means to extract a "voluntary" resignation from an infirm pastor. Protection was rooted rather in custom, and extended a little even beyond the grave. When a pastor died, the ministers of the neighboring churches acted as his pallbearers. These men, with whom he had sat in ecclesiastical councils and in less formal ministers' meetings, now each in turn preached one Sunday for his bereft church. And what the church would have paid a preacher or preachers for this period went instead to the pastor's widow.[4]

Such practices rested ultimately on the importance of the pastor to community solidarity. This is, in fact, what men realized when they faced the loss or lack of a pastor. When Stephen Farrar died in New Ipswich, New Hampshire, in 1809, a local judge is supposed to have warned, "Now there will be divisions." A female parishioner said much the same thing: "I am afraid there will be a division; we shall never again be united, as we have been in Mr. Farrar."[5] This theme turned up in other forms. When a congregation was looking for a new pastor, it sought a man "in whom we could be united." A minister warning a bereft parish against subsisting for too long without a pastor would insist that, lacking a pastor, the people would "assume the authority . . . of doing what is right in their own eyes," and thus fall into "contention and division."[6] During the emergence of Arminian and then Unitarian ideas at the end of the eighteenth century, the supposed bitterness of the doctrinal issues did not prevent an occasional church that was split on doctrine from remaining together under one pastor. Only after his death did the split become overt. And during the early years of the new century, an association of ministers that refused to define

heresy could serve this same function of postponing disunity.[7] These various responses rested on a common assumption: that the pastor functioned as symbol and core
of unity within the local group. Into him people could
project, and in him they could try to sink, their differences
about doctrine or social propriety or even about the sale
of lands. There was one difficulty, however: the same
sanction that made the pastor necessary to unity made the
pastoral relation vulnerable to any persisting trouble,
since its very persistence implied that the man was no
"real" pastor.

Just as local connection meant different things to members of different professions, so permanency meant different things to different denominations. In New England two
denominations were especially important, because they
competed with the Congregationalists and because they
shared in their own ways in the problems of ministerial
tenure: the Baptists from the seventeenth century on, and
the Methodists from the late eighteenth century. Baptist
principles in regard to ministers' terms did not differ
radically from Congregationalist principles. Within the
Baptists of New England there existed two fairly distinct
groups, one adhering to most aspects of congregational
polity, including an educated, paid ministry, and the other
going out of its way to find specialties such as foot washing
and an unpaid ministry that it could assert as the literal
demand of the Gospel. Even for this latter group, though,
an unpaid ministry meant indefinite tenure rather than
impermanent tenure. Because the minister had to make
his own living, he had to be a member of the local community; the deference given the usual Congregational
minister seems to have had its counterpart in the willingness of many a Baptist church to leave its ministry in the
hands of whoever was exercising it for the moment. Con-

jecturally, it seems likely that it was easy for the unpaid Baptist minister to pass his office to a son,[8] so that the unpaid Baptist ministry could tend to become the most permanent of all: hereditary status hardly tainted by origin in contract. While it is true that Baptists led the attack on Congregational privilege around 1800, they had themselves by then begun to veer away from sectarianism toward respectability,[9] and some Baptist groups began to experience the decline in ministerial tenure at about the same time as did Congregationalists.[10]

For both, part of the answer may come from the Methodists, since the collapse of permanency came at about the same time as the entry of Methodist influence into New England.[11] The ordained Methodist ministry was itinerant, and was required by the discipline of that church to be impermanent. Yet the Methodists had also local preachers, laymen who made their living in a community and who were licensed to preach there. Except for his lack of ordination, the lay preacher had a status much the same as that of the Baptist unpaid minister. The difference was made by the Methodist clergy proper, who were organized as a missionary group, ready to ignore any local rigidities. Whether it was they who were responsible for the disruption of permanency is open to question, but they did provide a model that other groups might follow when they entered the competition of domestic missions. Even during the stresses of the nineteenth century, traditional hierarchic organization like that of the Episcopalians made little appeal to the Congregationalists; it was the Baptist and Methodist examples that offered temptation.

THE POLEMIC BACKGROUND, 1699-1799

Not for some years, though, did Congregationalist ministers take careful account of the exact differences between

the types of ministers employed or produced by other denominations. Throughout the eighteenth century and into
the nineteenth, while they resented the intrusion of dis-
orderly preachers, they directed much of their analytical
worrying toward problems arising within the group of
orthodox clergy. Long before the Great Awakening, they
had worked out a set of standard explanations for difficulties between pastor and people, and these explanations
did in fact carry over into the nineteenth-century concern
for permanency.

To both Cotton Mather and John Wise, at the beginning
of the eighteenth century, clerical stability was the norm.
Their differences over church polity tend to conceal their
underlying agreement. Wise, using liberal arguments to
defend localism, found it expedient and probably congenial to insist that a pastor's status with his people was
typically so secure already that it needed no shoring up by
presbyteries or ministerial associations.[12] Mather, arguing
for a degree of centralization, and seeming to proceed from
authoritarian assumptions, found that ministerial stability
did not fit neatly into his scheme. Mather, the social "conservative" in modern terms, was actually pulling away from
the traditional order and toward something like denominationalism. He and those of like mind conceived of New
England Congregationalism, or at least of eastern Massachusetts Congregationalism, as an articulated organization,
which would protect the status of ministers as a group, and
which would differentiate among them by promoting the
more able to central, influential churches.

As in other matters, the Matherian position was ambiguous. It recognized certain valid reasons for ending a pastoral
relation. A minister might leave a church if he suffered
chronic illness, if his people subjected him to personal
harassment, or if dissension broke out between him and

his people. Additional reasons for his leaving included two that amounted to a justification of careerism: he might leave if the church denied him adequate subsistence, or if it were necessary for the "common good" of the "Catholick church."[13] In the latter case, the minister was not supposed to seek the move himself, but this rule could operate to encourage hypocrisy as easily as it could stability. On this issue, Mather tended toward caution and coyness. Noting that dissatisfaction arose whenever a church's only pastor wanted to leave, he observed that "some have thought the *public Benefit,* and *common Interest* of the Churches in general has not been so well consulted in this *perpetual confinement* of Grown and Bright Abilities."[14] Besides, the problem looked quite different when a move seemed to hurt, rather than benefit, the minister involved. Dissension between pastor and people might justify a council in advising his dismission, but the fact that a minister failed to achieve "success" in his pastoral work was specifically not recognized as a just cause for dismissal. And if the removal of a minister would create scandal—if, presumably, it would derogate from the general prestige of the clergy or the specific future work of that man—then such scandal might be a reason against removal.[15]

This last point is critical. Mather and those he endorsed were working to create a ministerial labor market within which ministers could be drawn toward the center of the market at Boston. They did not actually have that market, and they had to contend with prevailing standards according to which a minister was not mobile, and was presumed to be violating decency if he acted like a free bargaining agent. The Matherian view sought to promote a fluid, complex order, yet one that protected the authority and prestige of those who were the leaders for the time being.

Its opponents had the more difficult task, in the long run, of protecting a static, simple order; and John Wise among them found that a novel, liberal ideology served this conservative end.

By the end of the eighteenth century, these connections of idea with social stance had shifted. A series of controversies over ministerial tenure elicited increasingly sophisticated statements of how the ministry fitted into the larger social order. In some cases, controversy forced individuals to face up to the ambiguities in the earlier controversy between Wise and Mather. There were four main phases in the developments toward the end of the century: the Bolton, or Goss, controversy of the early 1770's; the pamphlet controversy between Peter Thacher and James Sullivan in the middle 1780's; the public efforts at ministerial cooperation by the Massachusetts clergy beginning in 1790; and the Ebenezer Chaplin case of 1791-1794.[16]

About 1770 a large part of the church in Bolton, Massachusetts, became dissatisfied with Thomas Goss, who had been settled as their pastor since 1741. They accused him of appearing in public while under the influence of liquor; as the wrangling over this accusation proceeded, they found occasion to charge him with duplicity and arrogance. Councils of ministers were called; these sided with Goss, but in 1771 the church and the town dismissed the minister in a unilateral action. Further councils were called, and a serious newspaper and pamphlet battle erupted; but Goss stayed dismissed despite being backed by most of the leading clergy of the province.[17] During this controversy, both sides indulged in much ordinary debate mongering, quarreling fatuously over the precise degree of Goss's arrogance, or over the meaning of punctuation in the Cambridge Platform, or over the applicability of Biblical proof texts to the case. In this, the partisans simply demonstrated their talents in behalf of special interest, but they also brought forward certain general conceptions of the ministry and of society.

On the most obvious level, this became a contention between "liberty" and "aristocracy" in church polity. Those who defended the right of the Bolton majority to dismiss their pastor republished the pamphlets that John Wise had written earlier in the century (This republication is the act for which the Bolton controversy has often been considered significant.) In reply, Nathaniel Whitaker, the Presbyterian minister of the Third Church in Salem, brought out a confutation of Wise. Arguing for councils and presbyteries as a form of polity, he exalted the role of aristocratic elements against either the democratic or the monarchic in any kind of government. He attacked the covenant as a basis of New England church government, insisting rather that any community was a corporate body simply because of its natural existence, without having to go through any formal process of establishment. To him, the existence of lines of authority between people was a part of natural growth not requiring any artificial justification. The rights that church covenants gave to the people violated the one absolute authority Whitaker did recognize, that of God over his elaborate creation.[18] Whitaker's views, while somewhat confined within formal political categories, began to show some of the viscous, organic conservatism that characterized much discussion of the ministry.

Most of the direct argument on the Bolton issue was carried by two clergymen: Ebenezer Chaplin, defending the right of the town to dismiss its minister whenever it wished, and Zabdiel Adams, defending Goss and the authority of the councils that backed Goss. Chaplin's argument was simple. Aligning himself with those who opposed the "growing power of the clergy," he questioned whether a council was any less subject to bias and self-interest than was a church or town. He presented a cut-and-dried economic analysis of the bargains between pastor and people, demonstrating that a town had no special interest in dismissing a minister (thereby incurring the obligation to pay a new settlement fee to its next minister, and losing much of the time over which the previous minister's settlement might have been amortized). Partly in order to protect himself against any charge that he was taking too cold-blooded an approach, Chaplin insisted that it was the minister, not the church, who often injected crass calculation into the pastoral relation: ministers were often guilty of covetous haggling, and in one case a minister had refused a generous grant of a farm and parsonage, alleging that they offered him not the ownership but only the use of the parsonage, conditional on his staying with them.[19]

If Chaplin had to protect his argument in this way, the necessity arose partly from Zabdiel Adams' attack on the relevance of precise economic analysis. Adams' views centered on a sensed opposition between Christian or social unity on the one hand, and individualism on the other. This explains the text that he chose for a sermon in Bolton: "Use not Liberty for an Occasion to the Flesh, but by Love serve one another. For all the law is fulfilled in one Word, even in this; — Thou shalt love thy Neighbour as thy self. But if ye bite and devour one another, take heed that ye be not consumed one of another" (Gal. v:13-15). To reinforce his emphasis on unity between minister and people, he recalled the traditional New England analogy of the pastoral relation to the bond between husband and wife: dissolvable, to be sure, but only under extreme circumstances and through proper forms. But the unity that Adams stressed was more than a set of bonds between different ranks and orders of men; it was a logical or organic unity, an underlying homogeneity of condition that made artificial any discussion of ranks, and that made abstract any economic analysis based on discrete units. Referring to the immediate problem of Goss's behavior, he said that in any controversy the propensity to rancor made it certain that both sides would soon share in blame. Besides, a minister was a person like his parishioners, liable to some of the same human weaknesses, and should not be held to an impossible priestly standard in either behavior or doctrine. And just as he was liable to passion, so his parishioners were liable to unreason. To Adams, Chaplin's argument that a people had no selfish interest in dismissing a minister rested on a narrowly economic conception of human nature, ignoring the range of passions that were just as much a part of motivation as any desire for lucre. To make clear what he thought of the ideology presented in Chaplin's anonymous pamphlets, he speculated about what Chaplin's occupation might be: perhaps he was an ordinary justice, who had picked up a smattering of law and with it more than a smattering of the pettifogging lawyer's narrow attitude toward life; or perhaps he was a minister who had left his charge and was trying to get others into the same condition.[20] Whether this hypothetical minister had been fired or had entered on a selfishly ambitious career, Adams did not specify; and either would suit his argument. As a whole, what Adams was saying was clear: the ministry was to be defended as part of a warm, textured, organic society, and those who attacked the rights of ministers represented a failure to participate that led to cold calculation and mutual destruction.

In addition to broad ideology, some particular problems about the profession arose in the Bolton controversy. The

Convention of Massachusetts Ministers, defending Goss, asked a humanitarian question: was it right to turn an old man out of his pastorate when he had no other support but public charity? And what effect would the precedent of Goss's dismissal have on future recruitment to the profession? Who would become ministers if that was the treatment they had to expect?[21] This practical worry over consequences spilled over into a similar controversy in Dorchester, Massachusetts, the same year (1773): a council considering a dispute between pastor and people there recommended the dismission of the pastor, but only after insisting that the minister retained his reputation and might be welcomed into pulpits elsewhere in New England.[22] In thus protecting the transferability of ministerial status when they knew popular opinion would question the transfer, the Dorchester council echoed the same worries that had beset Cotton Mather and his associates at the beginning of the century.

Incidents like those at Bolton and Dorchester cropped up often during the seventies and eighties, often turning on specific squabbles with little principle involved, but suggesting some larger issue. Thus, in 1783, a church in Bennington, Vermont, forced its minister out on what seemed a minor matter of polity: he was a regular Congregationalist, but the bulk of his church were Separate Congregationalists, who seemed to have settled him in a moment of desperation. The minister, David Avery, left, issuing pronouncements in favor of the "dignity of my office" and against the "levelling disposition" of the people; but the incident itself never rose above a tone of temperament and hairsplitting.[23] It remained for Peter Thacher, pastor in Malden, Massachusetts, not yet himself involved in any of the particular current pastoral difficulties, to lift such issues to general treatment in a pamphlet on the dismissal of clergymen. This pamphlet aroused a reply from James Sullivan, the libertarian politician and lawyer who during the eighties was working for the rights of dissenters as against the standing order.[24] Thacher issued a counter-argument, and the materials for a definition of views were thus available.

At bottom, the two men differed so completely in principle that argument could not even expose the ambiguities that united them. Thacher insisted that the pastorate was a vested contractual relation that neither party had a right to break without the consent of the other, unless upon the advice of a church council. On a practical plane, he argued that the minister was supposed to provide "counsels and instruction" to his people, which he could not consistently do if he was dependent on them.[25] Sullivan, on the other hand, believed that the people should avoid "servile awe" toward officeholders of any kind, whether magistrates or ministers. He accepted and recommended precisely the attitude that Thacher considered scandalous: that ministers were created such by the people, and should feel a proper sense of dependence.[26]

Within this clash of principle, the two men did carry the details of argument somewhat beyond the matters raised in Bolton in the previous decade. The Revolution had intervened, and this provided some material for argument. Both men accepted two ideas, that the Revolution had encouraged libertarian ideas in the people, and that the attendant inflation had undermined the value of ministers' incomes. They differed, of course, on how they evaluated the ideological change; and Sullivan argued that the churches had done as much as they could to make good the losses that ministers had suffered. He also used the notion of people's justice: many deposed ministers had been

Tories; and in those cases in which inflation had worked hardship on ministers, Thacher should have been moved by love of his country to find excuses for the inability of the churches to offer more relief. Thacher, refusing this Whig relativism, said that ministers deserved procedural justice even if they were Tories. Of course, when legalism favored Sullivan and pragmatism favored Thacher, the two men exchanged their bases of argument. Sullivan worked out a complex distinction between a minister's status as pastor to the church and his status as teacher to the parish; the right of the church to dismiss a pastor did not necessarily derogate from his claim to support by the parish. Here it became Thacher's turn to shrug off legalism, to argue that no concrete distinction could be made between the different aspects of a minister as a person, and to insist that he based his own argument on equity and humanitarianism.[27]

The critical point in the exchange came, not in any formal argument joined between the two men, but in two insinuations that Thacher suggested. While professing not to know the identity of the "J.S." against whom he disputed, Thacher made italicized efforts to put blame on lawyers for their incomes or for the Tories among them.[28] And questioning Sullivan's idea of parish support, Thacher asked whether the law was not tending rather to become an instrument for denying such obligations on all levels:

Mr. S. is thanked for the *delicate* manner in which he speaks of the *"wages"* of the clergy in his pamphlet and is desired to determine whether, in his opinion, a clergyman grown old and unfit for service and on this account dismissed by his people, hath a right to be maintained in the alms-house of the town, in common wtih the rest of its poor? The law used to oblige masters to maintain their servants; it is yet uncertain to some how far it is altered; it may not be improper therefore to ask Mr. S. whether the parish of which he was minister, or the town of which he was an inhabitant are obliged to maintain the said aged, dismissed, helpless minister?[29]

Thacher may have thought he was reducing the argument to the absurdity of comparing ministers and servants; actually, he showed thereby that he was arguing about the whole tone of society.

The point of view that Thacher defended merged into the efforts that Congregational ministers made in the 1790's to organize support for clerical status and for piety; and from this the particular concern for ministerial status flowed in a partly rationalized, sublimated form into the great revivalistic effort around the turn of the century. The stages in this process can be noted. In 1790 Congregationalist ministers meeting in convention at Boston adopted a recommendation that ministers and people require from preachers the necessary education and qualifications for their work, and that all ministers join the ministerial associations that could issue credentials to clergymen moving from one locality to another. This proposal led to correspondence between Congregationalist associations in the various New England states, and between Congragationalists and Presbyterians, looking to a general tightening of organization to benefit the status of ministers. Arguing in 1795 that "Divisions among ministers operate great injury to piety and religion," the Massachusetts convention could then move to the position in 1799 of calling for a "general revival of primitive Christianity"— without any open reference to the needs of clergymen.[30]

That the problems of clergymen continued, however, was shown by the fate of Ebenezer Chaplin, who in the Bolton case had defended the right of a people to dismiss their minister. Over the two decades after that case, he continued as pastor of the second church in Sutton, Massachusetts, reaching about the age that Goss had reached when he ran into trouble with his people. Now Chaplin found himself in a similar position. There may have been underlying strains, but acute difficulty began when he refused to let his daughter marry a parishioner. Whatever his motives—whether he disapproved of the suitor or perhaps had hoped for a better son-in-law than the local community could offer—he discovered that the rejected suitor was gaining allies. Soon the church wanted to dismiss the minister, and a council had to be called. The council advised dismission—but only if the church would compound its financial obligations to Chaplin. This the church refused to do, and Chaplin was out.[31] Chaplin then published a broadside over his signature, presenting his side of the particulars of the case.[32]

But the important polemic result was a long pamphlet on Congregationalism that took account of other cases besides Chaplin's, and that pushed the argument to a level as general as that taken by Peter Thacher in the 1780's. Chaplin, who had attacked ministerial prerogative earlier, and who had presumably endorsed the republication of John Wise's pamphlets in the Bolton case, was now defended by arguments that united the usual community orientation of conservatism with an appeal to the conservative undertone that had always been part of the way Wise wrote. In contrast to the earlier Presbyterian conservatism of Whitaker, the pamphlet stressed not only the covenant between pastor and church, but also the civil covenant and contract between parish and minister: "This also is for life, for it is so connected with the incorporating covenant of the Church, of which he is a member, and blended with his calling, which includes his local situation, that they cannot properly or consistently be separated;

he is a member of the body, and covenants to be such a member."[33]

From the authority of Wise as well as Hooker, the pamphlet drew the familiar analogy of the pastoral to the marital relation, not to be dissolved unless betrayed. If the right to break it at will were admitted, the result would be disaster; and by the 1790's it could be argued that such disaster was imminent.

The practice which is so prevalent, and growing at this day, of Minister and People making particular agreements about parting, on any other conditions, or in any other way, than the general plan of the Scriptures and Platform, is very improper, and a great evil. It is unsafe both for Minister and People. Many people seem to be fond of having it expressed in their settling a Minister, that he shall be dismissed when a major part or a major vote shall be against him. They must allow the same to the Minister. Such a precarious tenure is no settlement either of Minister or People, and must in its own nature keep Ministers and People perpetually fluctuating.

The Minister does not stand upon *good behavior,* but upon *pleasure;* he is therefore under a temptation to be a time-server, if he wishes to stay with the People: And at the same time he is also under a temptation to be plotting for a more promising place and employment; and prudence and duty will dictate, that he is always looking out and ready for a retreat. And in this case, if he has a proper forecast, he will see that he has a much larger salary that he may lay by for old age, or infirmity, when he is near past his labour . . . And this precarious scheme must in its own nature tend to breed jealousy between Minister and People; and it is inviting to restless, litigious minds, innumerable occasions to excite a party and dismiss a Minister in a heat; it may be, in revenge upon the Minister, or some other persons in the town or parish.[34]

At a time when the decline in permanency was just getting under way, this decline was thus predicted, and a specific mechanism of decline was suggested. The internal workings of church institutions, combined with natural human meanness, were a sufficient cause of any collapse that might come. In general, Chaplin's defense relied on the same attitudes expressed by other ministerial spokesman of that generation: a conservatism that was at once mellow and threatened, associating the good life with stability, and considering stability impossible if men had to calculate their welfare under the pressure of market dealing and original sin. And the shift in Chaplin's own position over this generation, together with the general rallying of clerical strength against the outside world, meant that the conservative argument came now to rely on those common impulses that in the Bolton case had been mere ambiguities uniting opponents.

MINISTERS' EXPLANATIONS OF THE DECLINE IN PERMANENCY

The explanation of the threat to permanency that was part of Chaplin's defense emphasized internal, structural problems, ignoring other, external factors such as the frontier and revivalism and denominational competition. Actually, the two classes of problems could not be kept separate. Congregationalists participated in the great revivalism that began toward the end of the 1790's. Some of this was an organizational reflex: they had begun home missions in the previous generation, sending men especially to the northern frontier of New England, and revivals were a natural extension of that work. Some of it arose from pressure to compete against vagrant preachers who, as the orthodox saw it, went about trying to "sow the seeds of religious discord, and disaffect the minds of people to a regular ministry."[35] This competition provided a link between frontier or revival problems and what happened inside an orthodox congregation. One writer for the Piscataqua Missionary Society, which was concerned with the New England frontier in the years just before 1805, made the connection nearly explicit. He described several ways in which a congregation might demonstrate its fickleness. There would be rich members who would take offense if the pastor paid too pointed attention to them; there would be the poor who would feel slighted by too little attention; and there would be some persons who would be drawn away by a "flaming preacher."[36] These rich and poor represented the aptness to dissension that the orthodox sensed as a form of original sin, while the sensational evangelist furnished a standard against which the dissident could measure a pastor, justifying any move to depose him.

For years these themes—the perversity of congregations, the mechanical destructiveness of a labor market, and the competitive demands of novelty—turned up as standard items in ministers' attempts to explain their misfortunes. The demand for novelty was felt at first to come mainly from the competition of "flaming" evangelists; it became institutionalized after a time in a sense that congregations hankered after whatever excitement they could get from ministers, that they tired quickly of any man who had been around for very long, that they wanted lively men who could both excite and organize, that they preferred always the young man to the mature. One Hopkinsian sympathizer delivered himself of sarcastic praise for the practice of conditional settlement, speaking as if for those who schemed against the intellectual followers of Samuel Hopkins: "In this way, we succeed in preventing the re-settlement of many ministers, who, before the events of these halcyon 'days of revivals' and 'benevolent exertions,' were considered very sound, evangelical and instructive." That the new men succeeded any better in revivals he did not believe; congregations ignored the man who had served long because they wanted one who was smart, popular, and young.[37]

Eventually this understanding of the problem of permanency produced a general explanation that reflected back upon the Bolton controversy of 1773. Moses Welch of New Haven noted particularly the effect of a people's demands on the preacher: "The disposition to discuss the literary qualities and fine abilities of the pastor is a prominent evil. Its tendency is to make the minister an essayist and the pulpit a theatre for oratorical display." But he set this observation within the idea that the people were coming to look on the minister less in the traditional, limited Congregational way and more as a priest on whom they could put special demands. They demanded, among other things, a peculiarly blameless life, different from that of his people—the demand, however justified, that had set off the Bolton controversy. And they put on the minister the burden for maintaining the growth of the church; if it failed to grow, they deduced that they needed "different preaching" or "a more active pastor." Not only that, but they exacted of the minister an excessive delicacy that inhibited him from discussing settlement terms and salary. It was precisely here, Welch felt, that the competitive advantage of the fashionable man was most dangerous: "the popular preacher who leaves the terms of his settlement wholly to his people, wrongs many of his brethren who cannot command a similar liberality, but who must in some measure conform to the fashion of settlement set by him."[38]

Eventually, in this controversy, ministers began to see complexities, or at least to concede complexities in order to make their basic complaints palatable to the lay public. With the self-castigation that came easily in the orthodox tradition, they noted that clergymen were themselves partly to blame for impermanency: even aside from complicity in careerism, ministers often failed to devote themselves to the scholarly ideal, thus depriving themselves of their best retreat from the frustrations of the social side of the ministry; many, accordingly, fled from churches because of relatively trivial vexations.[39]

From as early as 1810, and acutely from about 1830, a split developed in ministerial attitudes. Those who dominated Congregational affairs sought to advance the "cause" (whether in a generally religious, specifically evengelical, or narrowly denominational way) by increasing the recruitment of young ministers and sending a part of the new recruits into territory that would otherwise go unoccupied. Ministers were urged to bring pressure to bear on young men, and, more important, the various denominations established societies for giving scholarship aid to prospective ministers in college or seminary. This effort succeeded for a time, and the following generation brought a marked surge in recruitment. Probably no one objected to this phenomenon outright by arguing that the influx of new men would drive down standards for the old through job competition, but several writers got as close to this point as they decorously could. Daniel Dana, speaking to a principal recruiting society in 1818, insisted that too few men were going into the ministry, but urged caution:

Young men, preferring every thing else to *labor,* may seek a gratuitous support, and even the ministry itself, as a sanctuary for indolence. At this period, when religion excites an increased attention; when piety is, in some circles, *fashionable;* and when many species of Christian exertion, necessarily public, attract notice, and confer distinction, there is danger lest, from motives of pure *ambition,* some intrude themselves into the ministry. Against such applicants, our door must, if possible, be closed. While humble, unassuming piety—the piety which is

"Not obvious, not obtrusive, but *retir'd*,"
must be assiduously sought out and received under our fostering care.[40]

For some men, though, the fact that piety came from a
"retired" scene suggested danger rather than virtue. The
Unitarian John G. Palfrey believed that poor men were
quite capable of persuading themselves that they believed
in certain values if only those values offered them careers.
His mingled fears of social climbing and of religious
hypocrisy made him question

the claims of what are called Education Societies;—societies
which, finding a young man at the plough or in the work-shop
disposed to change his calling for that of a minister, take him
up, and carry him at little or no present expense to himself,
through all the steps of his preparation for that office. With
whatever caution administered, I should tremble to think
of the possible effect of such societies to provide a mercenary
ministry. To a young man in the humbler walks of industry,
becoming a minister appears to be bettering his condition;
and when this can be done chiefly at others' cost, the temptation cannot but be strong, and the minds of such be subjected
to a powerful bias to suppose themselves directed to this employment by a religious motive, when, if they examined more
closely, they might find it only a worldly calculation. I would
have our charity reserved from such an equivocal, not to say,
hurtful, use, for the assistance of those who have completed
their course of literary education. With such an education, a
person seems out of reach of the temptation to engage in the
ministry for the sake of advancing himself. It would be bold
to affirm that, in this country, where such prizes are held out
to talent and information, any well educated person betakes
himself to the ministry for the sake of a living.[41]

This was not simply the Unitarian snob speaking. Two
years after Palfrey expressed his fears, a writer in the orthodox, unashamedly anti-Unitarian magazine *Spirit of the
Pilgrims* defended an educated ministry against those who

argued that relaxation of standards was needed to expand
the number of ministers. He argued that education was
essential to permanency, since an uneducated man would
lack the equipment to keep either himself or his congregation long interested in what he had to say. He said, of
course, that high standards would not actually prevent an
increase in the ministerial population, but that was only
a qualification preceding his main point:

> Was it our sole object to fill any profession in life, to do so,
> we would make that profession as respectable and influential
> as possible . . . It is ministerial influence that is wanted, and
> that influence is by no means increased necessarily, as the
> number of ministers is augmented—the very contrary may be
> the case, and will be the case, if the increase is not of the right
> character. Burden the church with a multitude of unqualified,
> inefficient, unsuccessful ministers, and the very incubus of
> death is on her bosom.[42]

It would never do to maintain that there were too many
ministers—only that there were too many from some
short-range view or in relation to some special condition.
Thus it was that a writer in 1851 could look back on the
earlier surge in recruitment, note the ways in which both
it and mission activities generally were deprived of support by economic difficulties after 1837, and deduce that
"there may have been for a time an apparent surplus of
candidates for the sacred office. But foreseeing minds then
perceived, what had already begun to be realized, that the
time could not be distant when an alarming deficiency
must take the place of unusual abundance.[43]
Among the factors in the economic troubles at the end
of the thirties was one that ministers could and did discuss
without awkwardness, since it reflected nothing unfavor-
able on the ministry as such. This was the growing number
of "feeble churches" in New England, churches whose loss

of people and wealth made it difficult for them to support a regular ministry. If the influence of denominational competition on enfeeblement embarrassed a commentator, he could always take refuge in the general economic decline of rural New England. Clergymen could discuss impersonal economic problems without embarrassment, even if a few writing ministers did feel it necessary to warn their brethen against false delicacy in negotiating with congregations. As explanations for the decline in permanency, commentators cited especially the loss of parish lands and the effects of inflation. The two problems were related: loss of lands, or the organizing of new parishes without lands, deprived congregations of a resource from which they could compensate ministers; it also changed the composition of what the minister received. As a part-time farmer, whether he had worked the land himself or left that to hands, the pastor had got involved in the working life of his community and had derived much of his income in kind, partly invulnerable to changes in the price level. If he had to depend solely on salary or money contributions, he faced special difficulty in periods like the inflation of 1815-1819 or that of the middle thirties; the inability of congregations to appreciate this pressure meant "inadequate" salaries that led ministers to ask dismission and move on. From the minister's point of view, the congregation was served right if it then had to give a higher salary to his successor on the ground that "times have changed."[44]

The interpretations that ministers put upon the decline in permanency developed from a stage of immediate involvement, through a phrase in which new or shifting kinds of trouble helped to articulate the explanations, to a period of retrospective, academic survey of the decline. Up to about 1820, only seers thought of the decline as a mass phenomenon; people wrote more about particular tensions or breaks in the pastoral relation. By the 1830's and 1840's, they saw the movement whole and were inclined to focus it in terms of immediate issues that broke the relation: inflation, denominational quarrels, or "exciting discussions on questions of moral reform." At the end of the 1840's, they were hoping that reform agitation had died down, and this hope became sometimes a longing after the older New England way.[45] Three synthesizing views emerged. On the orthodox side, Timothy Tuttle of Ledyard, Connecticut, combined belief in latent instability with a historical labeling of the trigger that released latency. He dated frequent dismission from the late eighteenth century or the years around 1800. That had been a period both of revivals and of "discriminating doctrinal preaching." The demanding theology of Jonathan Edwards' disciples aroused a restive opposition, some dismissions resulted, and thus the disaffected learned how easily they could manipulate a pastor into leaving. Dismissions became more frequent even though the amount of disaffection was not necessarily greater than it had been during the days of permanency.[46]

Tuttle's simple pessimism did not characterize all the orthodox. Nathaniel Bouton, writing about New Hampshire ministers, proceeded systematically. He attempted to calculate just how much permanency had declined, and he catalogued the reasons for the decline in permanence: (1) the loss of parsonage lands caused by the rise of Unitarians, who laid claim to them; (2) the "example and influence" of ministers of other denominations, who opposed the standing order and desired change; (3) the "increase of feeble churches," with "the law of self-preservation as well as desire for greater usefulness, operating on the pastors to induce removal"; (4) "a change in the manners and habits of society generally, which pays less respect to age, office, and authority of every kind"; and (5) "the want, in some cases, of that liberal and complete education which places ministers on an equality of standing and influence with educated men in other professions, and enables them to feed the people with understanding and knowledge; a want, which when discovered by the more discerning, and by the majority of a people, no other qualities can supply."[47] No academic could ask more in the way of plural causation; all that united Bouton's separate points was a sense that the minister had been deserted and attacked, that he was himself to blame only as he deserted the ideal of what he had once been.

Twenty years later, a liberalizing Unitarian, Joseph H. Allen, provided an interpretation similar to Bouton's, but more sophisticated in tone: precise where Bouton had been evasive, philosophically evasive where Bouton had been precisely querulous. Though he used the lengths of ministers' terms as his ultimate criterion, he put most of his discussion in terms of the supplanting of the old order by the "voluntary system" of ministerial support. Where Bouton had grounded his discussion on an analysis of term lengths, Allen sought the "definite point" of "visible transition" at which the old order became no longer tenable. He found it, in Massachusetts, in the legal disestablishment of the Congregational and Unitarian churches in 1833. The change had been inevitable because of "diversities in population and interest," because of "widening differences of creed," and because of the "progress of a theoretical republicanism." Once set in motion, the voluntary system developed a built-in instability, supported by features taken over from the rest of society. From the political sphere ministers took the "vice of office-hunting," and churches took the "clamor for rotation." Within the churches trying to live on the voluntary system, financial problems interfered with ministerial support. The system emphasized the differential personal attributes of ministers, and sectarianism increased the standards of competing display while cutting the constituency of each congregation. In contrast to those ministers who kept hoping that permanency would stop declining and turn upward again, Allen concluded that ministerial terms were likely to become shorter instead of longer. He could accept this conclusion because he had himself come to favor the idea of a specialized ministry, itinerating between churches that would be organized as elaborate community centers.[48] His cheerful pessimism about the outlook for permanency mirrored in reverse the way that the orthodox conducted their discussion of the subject: they usually embedded their explanations in a flow of piety, and concluded that the only real hope for a return to permanency lay in creating a new state of mind in both minister and people.[49]

EMPIRICAL DATA ON PERMANENCY: THE NEW HAMPSHIRE CASE

The variety of explanations the ministers offered, and the obviousness of the special pleading in some cases, make out of all these contemporary explanations a set of questions, each of the form: did such-and-such a phenomenon actually operate to reduce permanency? Part of the answers to these questions can come from an analysis of data on the lengths of ministers' terms in office. The data are available in three forms: in the annual lists of ministers that associations or conventions of ministers published, especially during the early part of the nineteenth century; in the retrospective lists of all ministers within particular areas, published by historical-minded denominations from the 1830's on; and in Frederick Lewis Weis's genealogically oriented lists published much later by the Society of the

Descendants of the Colonial Clergy. Such lists are not completely satisfactory. In most cases, a list will cover only the men of a particular denomination; data on rival denominations for the same period may or may not be available. Or a list may cover all the activities of a group of men within one state, but leave uncovered those parts of careers spent outside the particular state; in such a case, the data furnish no sense of the whole career patterns of individuals. Neither of these faults can be laid to the publications of the Society of the Descendants of the Colonial Clergy; there, it is the inherent cutoff at 1776 that limits the usefulness of the gathered information. After all, the collapse of permanency had its roots in the late eighteenth century, becoming a painful, unavoidable issue only in the nineteenth. Yet taken together, these several batches of information yield overlapping, interlocking groups of precise information, thus establishing the main lines in a picture of the changing structure of the clerical profession. Because the different segments of the profession were interrelated, either through common ideals or through a common labor market, any necessary interpolation should be fairly reliable.

Probably the longest single run of data available is that in Henry A. Hazen's *Congregational and Presbyterian Ministry and Churches of New Hampshire* (Boston, 1875). Hazen, an antiquarian and denominational partisan, tabulated the following information on each of 1143 ministers from the 1630's to 1875: place and date of birth, date of death, education (college, private theological instruction, or seminary), date of appointment to a particular church, how that term began (that is, whether by ordination, installation, or supply), date of dismission, and length of term. For each church Hazen included the date of formal gathering, something of organizational history (noting es-

pecially mergers, extinctions, and changes of denomination), and the 1870 population of the town where the
church was located. From his listing of ministerial terms
Hazen excluded all those that lasted less than one year;
this might overstate somewhat the average level of permanency, but there is no reason to think that such an
omission would change even the details of the continuing
picture.

Hazen's data are, of course, limited to New Hampshire
and to one denomination. (The Presbyterians in the collection are few, and were essentially tolerated interlopers
within the Congregational fold, following the same cus-
toms and showing the same statistical characteristics as the
mass within which they lived.) The limitation to New
Hampshire is not, however, so serious as it might appear.
The state provided a fair sample of all kinds of New England communities outside metropolitan Boston: established
coastal towns, interior isolated towns, interior river towns,
and farther frontier regions that opened up only late in
New England history. Within the range of patterns that
Congregationalism assumed in the United States over the
nineteenth century, New Hampshire stood almost midway.
Neither as conservative in its treatment of ministers as
Massachusetts and Connecticut, nor as loosely modern as
Congregationalists in the Middle West, the state had a proportion of settled ministers in 1877 that was nearly as low
as the national average (though this average was approxi-
mated more closely yet by Maine and Vermont).[50]

In their thinking, New Hampshire Congregationalists
may have been conservative, for the New Hampshire Association of Ministers was the only state association that
resisted the calling of the Congregational National Council
in 1865.[51] But as a population group they reflected both

the older pattern and the pressures undermining that pattern.

In New Hampshire, the average term that a minister served a church was at first low, in the generation after settlement in the 1630's. (See Graph 1.) Not until the 1650's did the average of terms beginning in a decade exceed ten years, and not until the seventies did it pass twenty years, thus reaching the level "typical" of the colonial period. During all this time, of course, settlement in the province had not moved much beyond a few towns near the coast or near Massachusetts. By the time deeper settlement got under way in the first generation of the eighteenth century, ministerial tenure was fixed at a high level. Although a moderate drop in term levels in the middle of the century reflected the disorders of the Great Awakening, terms continued to be long until 1785 or after. They sagged a bit in the 1790's but still reached remarkably high levels in 1790 and 1804—about thirty and twenty-five years respectively, for the terms beginning in those years. (See Graph 2.) The real break came abruptly in 1807. After 1806, there were no two successive years in each of which beginning terms averaged more than ten years; after 1808, there was no single year in which beginning terms averaged as high as twenty. Despite this abruptness, the collapse of permanency took about a generation to work through as a process. Only after 1821 was there no year in which beginning terms averaged over ten years. And during this entire period, the survival of many ministers with long tenures from the old days gave an ambiguous tone to the profession as a social group. Not until about 1822 did the average of terms *ending* in any particular year begin to drop seriously, and this average did not reach a low level of less than ten years until 1837. After 1837, the average of

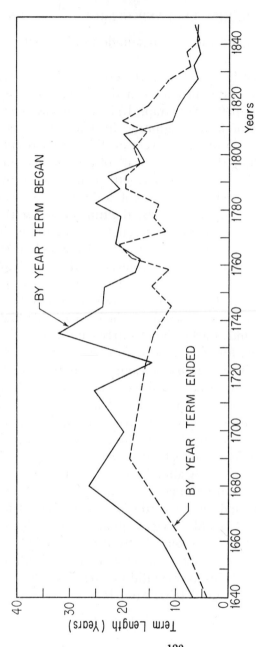

GRAPH 1. New Hampshire Congregational and Presbyterian clergy, average term lengths. In this graph, terms are averaged over periods of five years or longer, depending on the quantity of data available at various periods. Calculated by the years in which terms began, lengths tend to reflect the kind of contractual understandings into which ministers and churches were entering in each year. Calculated by the years in which terms ended, they tend to reflect the timing of conditions that interrupted ministerial terms. (*Source:* Hazen.)

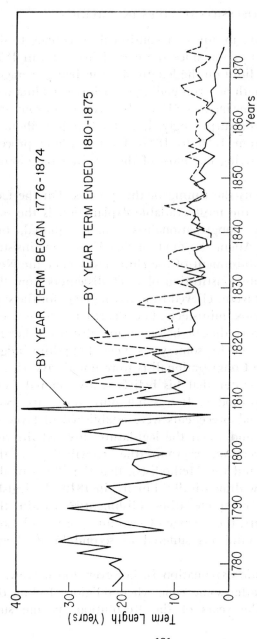

GRAPH 2. New Hampshire Congregational and Presbyterian clergy, average term lengths, by single years. Beginning in the late eighteenth century, there were enough terms beginning or ending in any one year to permit the presentation of meaningful single-year curves. Simply for visual clarity, the curve by year term ended is omitted before 1810. (*Source:* Hazen.)

121

terms beginning in any year continued, of course, to decline in Hazen's data, since the end of his series in 1875 puts an upper limit on the length of terms being averaged in. But the length of terms ending in each year maintained a steady level, varying sporadically between about four and eight years. Not surprisingly, it had taken just about a generation—from 1806 to 1837—for the whole process of collapse to wring out most of the survivals of colonial practice.

What explains the timing of this process? On the face of the matter, the most available explanation is the one that orthodox Congregationalists usually ignored, but which Joseph Allen, the modernizing Unitarian, insisted on: the disestablishment of the churches. Under the New Hampshire state constitution of 1792, dissenters from the standing order were relieved from paying taxes for the support of orthodox ministers. The dissenter was obliged, however, to prove that he belonged to a distinct, other religious group; and for some years New Hampshire judges friendly to the Congregationalists were not always willing to grant a dissenter that his beliefs really differed from those of the orthodox. It was not until the years 1803-1807, when legal precedents were established in favor of the dissenters and when the legislature directed the recognition of several major groups (the Freewill Baptists, the Universalists, and the Methodists), that the effects of the law could show dramatically. Finally, in 1819, the legislature enacted complete disestablishment:[52] within the next three years, the average of beginning terms for Congregationalist ministers suffered its second break downward.

This legalistic explanation is, however, too narrow. It assumes that after some time when religious feeling declined—say, the years of the Revolution—people sup-

ported orthodox ministers only because they were required
to do so by law. It assumes a restive people, straining at
the bonds of oppression. It assumes, too, that the dissenters
shared in no significant way in the ideal of a settled ministry bound in the life of the community. None of these assumptions is fully justified. Compare the case of Rhode
Island. There, Congregationalism was never established,
never even had a particularly dominant place in the community. If the Congregationalists were strong in some
towns and in some social groups, they still did not control
the state government. The pastor of any particular church
depended on the voluntary support given him by his local
people. In 1840 the *American Quarterly Register* published
a historical table of Congregational ministers in Rhode
Island, similar in style to Hazen's later register for New
Hampshire, though less full in detail.[53] The same pattern
emerges as in New Hampshire. (See Graph 3.) Through
the first quarter of the eighteenth century, the beginning
and ending term lengths were highly mixed. They reached
a firm, high level from 1731 to 1805, when they broke
sharply downward, with a predominance of very short
terms from 1815 or 1823 on. Again, a logical lag shows in
the lengths of terms *ending* in each year, but the available
data suggest that this measure reached a very low level of
from two to four years in 1836. Quite clearly, congregations could grant long tenures without any legal compulsion, and when they decided to stop giving such tenures,
they followed a process that could be much the same
whether it started from a compulsory or from a voluntary
regime.

Certain circumstances might conceivably save the importance of legal change as an explanation of the collapse
of permanency. As will appear from other data, the Congregational churches of New England were in the proc-

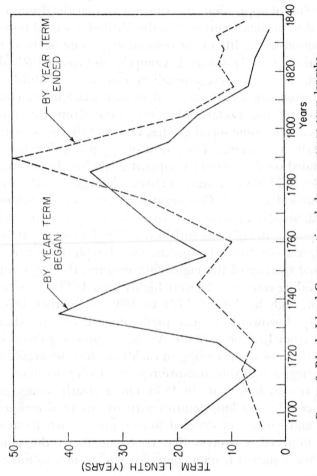

GRAPH 3. Rhode Island Congregational clergy, average term lengths. (Source: *American Quarterly Register*, 1840.)

ess of becoming a single, articulated, internally differentiated labor market. It may appear that the phased withdrawal of legal support from the clergy in Massachusetts,
Connecticut, and New Hampshire set up an environment
in which the Congregational clergy of Rhode Island had
to participate. If, just over the state line, dismissed ministers were looking for new churches, and destitute churches
were looking for new ministers, how could Rhode Islanders avoid being drawn into the competitive pressure?
That Rhode Island Congregationalists were an isolated
minority would only reinforce their tendency to go along
with the practice of their strong fellow communicants in
nearby states. Still, there are difficulties with this explanation. There is no compulsion by which a fast-moving labor
market must automatically break down the torpor of an
adjoining slow market, as long as the employers and work-
ers in the slow market are willing to maintain their bargains and their slow pace. And even if the Rhode Islanders
had been drawn into impermanency by the example or
the economic compulsion of other states, there should have
been a lag between the stages in growing impermanency in,
say, New Hampshire and the corresponding stages in
Rhode Island. In fact, the chronology of the collapse was
almost precisely the same in the two areas. Any mechanical
transmission connecting the Rhode Island market with the
rest of New England must have been efficient, indeed.

The comparison between two kinds of Congregationalists—those established in New Hampshire and those not
established in Rhode Island—can be matched with a
comparison between two New Hampshire denominations:
the established Congregationalists and the nonestablished
Baptists. There exists for the Calvinistic Baptists of New
Hampshire, who were the dominant Baptist group in the
state until well into the nineteenth century, a register of

ministerial terms to 1836, similar to the data presented by Hazen and the *American Quarterly Register*.[54] For the decade of the 1770's through the 1820's it lists 113 terms of definite length; these form the curve that is superimposed on comparable curves for New Hampshire and Rhode Island Congregationalists in Graph 4. The basic facts are the same for all three groups: the long terms of the middle or late eighteenth century, the break downward near the end of the century, and the achievement of very short terms by the 1820's or 1830's. Among the three groups, term lengths for the New Hampshire Congregationalists began to decline last and most slowly; legal establishment may well have retarded the decline for a time. But disestablishment was not a necessary step in the destruction of permanency. More likely, the same influences that undermined the legal basis of the standing order worked directly on the churches, breaking down both the desire to maintain permanency and the will to resist legal change. If they suffered calamity, it was a calamity in which they conspired.

If the lifting of political restraint offers no major explanation, neither do some obvious geographical explanations. The "frontier" explains some things. Terms were short in the first years of settlement in the seventeenth century; and terms were also short in the initial decade of settlement for some, but not all, of the New Hampshire counties settled in the eighteenth century. In almost every county, terms were few during the first fifty years after settlement, and varied widely in length. But if the frontier had any lasting effect, then one or both of two phenomena should have appeared. Ministerial terms should have averaged consistently lower in the new, more northerly counties during some significant period, or the break downward in term lengths should have begun earlier in the

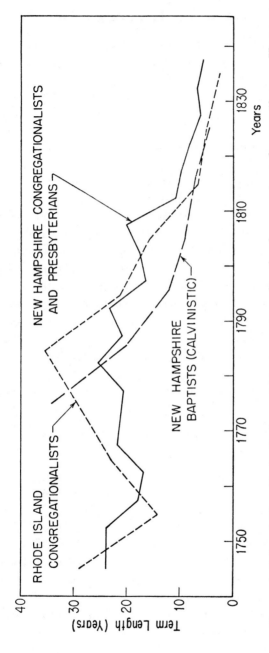

GRAPH 4. Selected New England clergymen, average term lengths, by year term began. (*Source: Hazen; American Quarterly Register, 1840; Ebenezer E. Cummings, Sermon, 1835.*)

young counties, then have spread to the older areas. Nothing of the sort happened. (See Table 1.) In all the frontier counties, terms reached the typically high level by at least the second decade of settlement, and thereafter maintained that level at least as firmly as terms in the older counties. In none of the frontier counties did term lengths break downward significantly earlier or later than in established counties. Unless the frontier phenomenon acted through changes in denomination, it had no relation to ministerial tenure. Change of denomination, as from Congregational to Baptist, was certainly important on the frontier; still, it is hard to imagine the frontier having critical influence and not causing changes within Congregational ranks.

Similarly, localism or "home-townism" in a minister's career seems to have had no bearing on permanency. If the terms are classified according to whether the minister was born in the same county as the church, or born somewhere else in New Hampshire, or born somewhere else in New England, or born outside New England altogether, only one difference between these four groups emerges, as to term length or the chronology of changes in term length. (See Graph 5.) Men coming from outside New England did average markedly shorter terms until the 1840's; presumably they often arrived only after maturity, and therefore had less time left to spend on the local ground. The larger negative result, though, is so surprising as to be significant. Much of what contemporary argument said about the New England ministers, much also of what later interpreters have felt about New England society, has tended to emphasize the organic nature of the community, and of the local church as the core of those graced within that community. The minister was a member of that church, and presumably shared its organic life. But if this were the whole story, then those churches in which the

Table 1. Average term lengths, by county.

County	First year of decade in which term began											
	1630	1640	1650	1660	1670	1680	1690	1700	1710	1720	1730	1740
Rockingham	9.7	9.0	23.3	3.0	38.0	—	16.0	29.0	19.5	14.8	32.7	25.8
Strafford	2.3	7.5	7.5	—	9.0	31.0	—	—	25.7	—	42.5	17.5
Hillsborough						23.0		4.5	19.0		33.0	27.0
Merrimack									67.0		41.5	15.0
Cheshire											9.5	7.0

County	1750	1760	1770	1780	1790	1800	1810	1820	1830	1840	1850	1860
Rockingham	28.8	18.1	21.1	22.6	17.0	15.8	13.3	6.8	5.6	6.9	5.1	3.9
Strafford	12.5	11.0	13.0	24.7	11.0	30.0	7.4	2.8	6.4	8.3	4.1	3.6
Hillsborough	12.7	29.9	19.3	35.5	31.6	16.8	8.3	9.4	6.2	6.1	5.2	3.4
Merrimack	7.5	11.1	20.0	23.9	26.3	26.3	13.5	7.1	8.1	5.8	4.3	4.1
Cheshire	15.0	21.8	20.5	21.9	24.2	24.4	10.3	7.2	4.6	6.3	3.5	3.3
Sullivan	2.0	24.5	9.7	23.2	9.0	11.3	10.3	7.8	5.8	8.5	4.3	3.3
Belknap		10.0	39.0	—	6.0	31.5	5.5	4.7	7.5	6.5	5.5	3.7
Grafton		18.7	21.5	12.0	18.3	17.0	8.8	7.2	5.3	6.9	3.4	3.7
Carroll			38.0	50.0	29.5	2.0	—	10.6	5.7	4.9	4.7	3.8
Coos					28.0	—	4.0	2.0	3.2	4.7	3.0	3.8

Source: Hazen.

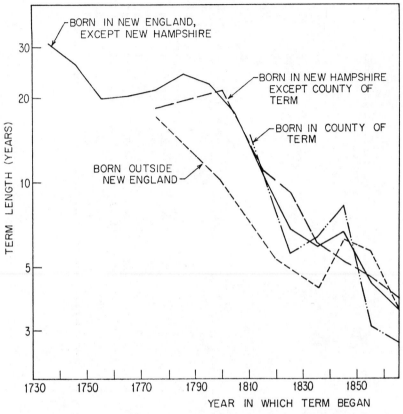

BORN IN NEW ENGLAND,
EXCEPT NEW HAMPSHIRE

BORN IN NEW HAMPSHIRE
EXCEPT COUNTY OF
TERM

BORN IN COUNTY OF
TERM

BORN OUTSIDE
NEW ENGLAND

TERM LENGTH (YEARS)

YEAR IN WHICH TERM BEGAN

GRAPH 5. New Hampshire Congregational and Presbyterian clergy, average term lengths, by relation of minister's birthplace to county where he served his term. (*Source:* Hazen.)

identity of minister and community was closest should have shown some resistance to the collapse of permanency.

The fact that explains away this touch of paradox is simple. At no time from the seventeenth century on did more than a minor fraction of New Hampshire Congregational churches have ministers who had been born in New Hampshire, and at almost no time did more than a still

smaller fraction have ministers born in the same county
as the church. (See Table 2.) The minister, far from being

Table 2.   Percentage distribution and number of terms,
1630-1875, by relation of minister's birthplace
to location of term.

	Minister's birthplace				
Decade, by first year	Outside New England (per cent)	New England, outside New Hampshire (per cent)	New Hampshire, outside county of term (per cent)	County of term (per cent)	Total terms in decade (number)
1630	100	—	—	—	6
1640	100	—	—	—	3
1650	100	—	—	—	5
1660	100	—	—	—	2
1670	50	50	—	—	2
1680	—	100	—	—	2
1690	—	50	—	50	4
1700	14	86	—	—	7
1710	9	91	—	—	11
1720	20	60	—	20	5
1730	12	71	—	17	24
1740	10	71	5	14	21
1750	—	89	11	—	18
1760	12	81	7	—	43
1770	2	92	4	2	50
1780	8	77	11	4	48
1790	10	79	9	2	57
1800	7	61	17	15	54
1810	3	69	17	9	58
1820	3	72	15	10	116
1830	7	61	20	12	223
1840	5	59	27	9	225
1850	5	57	25	13	259
1860	9	65	22	5	235
1870-1875	21	57	15	7	60

Source: Hazen.

a "real" member of the local community was usually a
stranger. It is true, of course, that a son might succeed his
father in a church. Otherwise, though the relation between

minister and church may have been a quasi-marital relation, it was marriage on an exogamous pattern. How this
came about is plain to see. When a man finished his education, the chance of a position falling open in any church
known to him was slight, especially during the earlier
period when pastors' terms lasted a lifetime. Unless he had
a particularly close connection in the pastorate of his own
community, he would have to look elsewhere. His looking
elsewhere then used and reinforced the defined nature of
the New England pastorate: an organic relation created by
artifice, the artifice being the contract of settlement. A
meaningful contract requires that the two parties be independent of each other. This they were. Pastoral "exogamy"
meant, moreover, that ministerial authority, while exercised by someone who had plenty of time to become
familiar with his local people, was exercised by a man who
usually moved at a psychological distance from them, who
was not involved in their affairs. It served the same function that was supposedly served by the marriage practices
of European royalty, of keeping the circles of authority
somewhat detached from the spheres of the governed.

Localism seems, if anything, to have been associated
with periods of evangelism, settlement, or heavy ministerial
recruitment. In only two decades, the 1830's and 1840's,
were more than a third of the ministers who began terms
men who had been born anywhere in New Hampshire.
These decades were a period of forced recruitment, during
which many men presumably served what amounted to
short trial ministries in New England before moving west
to supply newly established churches. Impermanency and
a heavy turnover also provided an opportunity for work
near home that had not existed before.

On certain explanations—disestablishment, the frontier,
and localism—the New Hampshire and Rhode Island data

present negative testimony. They undercut the adequacy of any of these factors as a cause of permanency or impermanency. More positively, the data serve to define the mechanisms through which (not because of which) the change took place, and to define some of the meanings of change. The important variables, of those available in Hazen, are education, age, and kind of tenure.

During the latter part of the eighteenth century, certain categories of ministers did have terms just about as low as those that came with the break after 1805: men who were not installed; men who were serving unstable, insecurely planted churches; and men with little or no higher education. The one factor that was most consistently associated with short terms was lack of installation. (See Graph 6.) No matter how much education a man had, or what kind, if he served a church as what came to be called a "stated supply" he could not and probably did not expect to stay for long. Among those who served on supply, even education did not carry with it a relative advantage in term length. This meant, simply, that churches took seriously the formalities of ordination and installation, either being constrained by the obligation once incurred or avoiding the obligation if the intention to observe it was not there. Although the terms of installed pastors declined at the beginning of the nineteenth century in much the same pattern as those of the whole ministerial population, churches became less inclined to use the form of tenure that was inappropriate to short terms. Especially after the 1820's or 1830's, the proportion of noninstalled ministers began to increase sharply. In this, New Hampshire churches participated in what was happening to Congregationalists in the nation generally. By the late 1850's, when the *Congregational Quarterly* began to gather and publish national statistics, the number of settled pastors had reached a

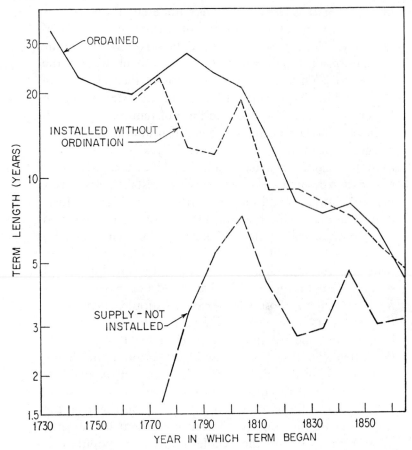

GRAPH 6. New Hampshire Congregational and Presbyterian clergy, average term lengths, by form of tenure. (*Source:* Hazen.)

stable figure of about 900 that fluctuated only slightly over the following two decades; but during those same decades the number of nonsettled Congregational ministers in the country continued to increase, from about 600 in 1856 to about 1800 in 1876.[55]

While supply increased in relative importance over the

last two generations covered by Hazen's data, another category that had a similar relation to term length became necessarily less important. This was instability in the life history of the local church, as measured by a church's suffering some major change at any time before 1875, such as extinction, change of denomination, or merger with another church. There were enough terms served at churches in the first two categories to permit a systematic comparison with the term lengths of ministers serving the stable churches that survived essentially unchanged from their organization until 1875. (See Graph 7.) The curves for unstable churches never cross that for stable churches, even though they do approach it closely in certain decades. Of course, the number of terms in churches that later became extinct is very small for the later decades, so that full comparison is possible only through the 1850's. But the fact that terms in unstable churches were consistently lower than those in stable churches permits the distinction to be used in the same way as that between settled pastors and stated supplies. Whenever some other, more ambiguous distinction is analyzed, the factors of church life history or of tenure form can be abstracted out, making it possible to observe the ambiguous factor with greater precision. This kind of analysis is particularly useful when applied to the education of ministers.

First, though, a difficulty interferes with any evaluation of the relation of different kinds of education to term lengths. The kinds of education available to prospective ministers shifted through three phases. College education was available through the whole period, and most of the ministers serving at any time had graduated from college, whether Harvard in the early years or, commonly, Dartmouth in the later years. But until the latter part of the eighteenth century prospective ministers did not as a

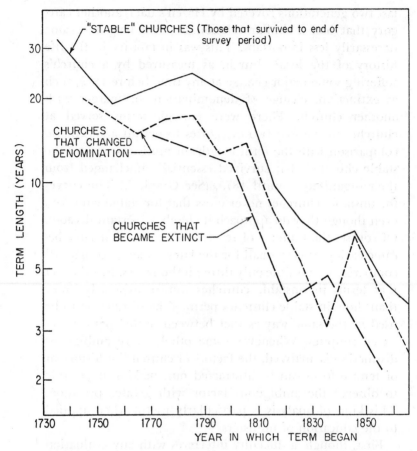

GRAPH 7. New Hampshire Congregational and Presbyterian clergy, average term lengths, by life history of church served. (*Source:* Hazen.)

rule get any formal, distinctly professional education. Then, from about 1770 to about 1840, a major part of the ministers served a professional apprenticeship by reading theology in the household of an older minister. A third stage came after 1800, especially after about 1820, when

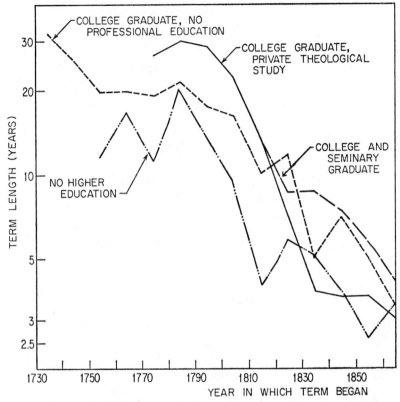

GRAPH 8. New Hampshire Congregational and Presbyterian clergy, average term lengths, by selected types of education. (*Source:* Hazen.)

most ministers had attended one of the new theological seminaries, such as Andover. At any particular time, the ministers who had had one of the then older kinds of education would tend to be an older group, and thus would have less time left to spend in a term even under the most permanent of conditions. The terms of such an older group would seem unusually long if measured by the average time they had already been in office at their present churches,

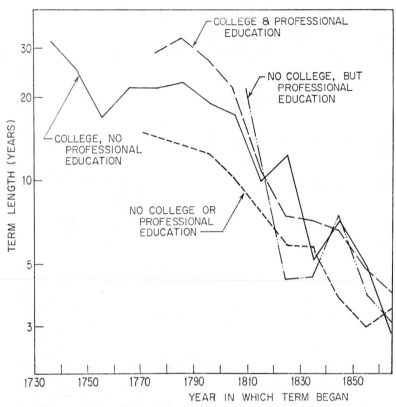

GRAPH 9. New Hampshire Congregational and Presbyterian clergy, average term lengths, by type of education of ministers serving "stable" churches. (*Source:* Hazen.)

but unusually short if measured by the average length of new terms they were then beginning. This artifact shows on the simplest comparisons of term lengths by type of education. (See Graph 8.) A general pattern is clear. Men with no higher education averaged short terms. College graduates who had had no professional education averaged longer terms. And college graduates who had gone on to get the latest form of professional education averaged (ex-

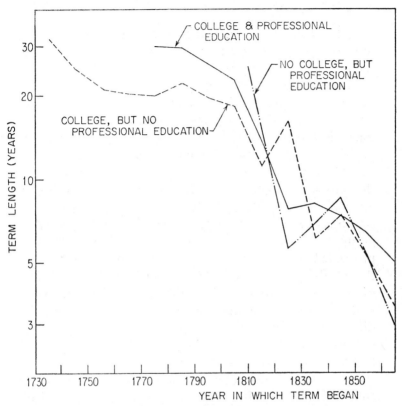

GRAPH 10. New Hampshire Congregational and Presbyterian clergy, average term lengths of settled ministers, by type of education. (*Source:* Hazen.)

cept in the 1820's) the longest terms of all. And in a rough way (see above, Graphs 9 and 10) men with professional education but without college followed a pattern like that of the men with college but without professional education. There is one great flaw in the pattern: from the 1830's on, college graduates with private theological education averaged very low beginning terms. This is almost entirely an effect of the aging of this particular group of

139

men. In 1830, for instance, these men averaged 16.4 years in office—the most "permanent" educational group among the ministers in that year.

In some ways, Table 3 presents a more realistic picture of the shifting ministerial population than Graph 8. This population was never very large, and never much greater than the 180 it reached in 1860. It rarely included at any one time more than two different educational groups large enough to permit statistical comparison. As late as 1770, the only large group within the whole was men who had graduated from college but had not had any professional training. A generation after that, this was still the largest group, but it was almost equaled in size by those who had proceeded from college to private theological study. Although these latter had been in office for a shorter period of years, both groups had on the average been in office without break from the normal age of ordination; the difference in terms was, therefore, only a reflection of the difference in ages. By this time, though, the group that had had no higher education at all was large enough for comparison; although almost exactly the same age as the college graduates without professional education, it had an average term only a fourth as long.

In 1830, after the lapse of another generation, there were three large educational groups; each consisted of college graduates, the difference being between those without professional education, those who had done a private apprenticeship, and those who had graduated from seminary. By this time, those who had had private theological study had been in office somewhat longer than those without professional education, yet were a slightly younger group. The seminary graduates had terms only a third as long, but then they were almost twenty years younger as a group. Actually, of the three groups, only the young

Table 3. Principal characteristics of ministerial population, for five selected years, by type of education.

Education	1770			1800			1830			1860			1875		
	No.	Avg. term to date (years)	Avg. age	No.	Avg. term to date (years)	Avg. age	No.	Avg. term to date (years)	Avg. age	No.	Avg. term to date (years)	Avg. age	No.	Avg. term to date (years)	Avg. Age
No higher ed.	5	6.0	40.4	14	4.4	47.8	7	3.1	41.6	7	2.3	49.0	12	2.9	47.2
Coll. grad.; no prof'l. ed.	63	15.2	48.7	59	16.8	47.4	25	13.4	55.7	12	15.6	57.7	6	5.9	46.3
Coll. nongrad.; no prof'l. ed.	—	—	—	—	—	—	—	—	—	—	—	—	1	0	50.0
Pvt. theol. study; no coll.	1	34.0	60.0	1	17.0	52.0	9	6.9	36.8	9	8.2	52.8	7	7.1	45.3
Coll. grad.; pvt. theol. study	4	9.8	37.3	41	12.7	42.1	50	16.4	52.1	8	7.4	60.4	3	3.3	54.7
Coll. nongrad.; pvt. theol. study	—	—	—	1	1.0	28.0	5	5.0	41.4	2	15.5	57.0	—	—	—
Sem. nongrad.; no coll.	—	—	—	—	—	—	1	4.0	47.0	—	—	—	4	0.8	37.0
Coll. grad.; sem. nongrad.	—	—	—	—	—	—	7	2.1	37.3	9	6.4	48.0	6	5.2	54.2
Coll. nongrad.; sem. nongrad.	—	—	—	—	—	—	—	—	—	2	1.0	38.5	1	0	46.0
Sem. grad.; no coll.	—	—	—	—	—	—	7	2.1	33.9	34	5.9	48.2	20	3.2	46.8
Coll. and sem. grad.	—	—	—	2	19.5	49.0	34	5.4	36.4	97	7.3	45.3	89	5.0	46.1
Sem. grad.; coll. nongrad.	—	—	—	—	—	—	1	1.0	32.0	—	—	—	5	1.2	34.8
Totals	73			118			146			180			154		

Source: Hazen.

seminary graduates had been serving in their present charges since near the usual ordination age. By 1830, permanency had so far collapsed that no large group that had been working in the profession for long was still serving in the same churches they began in. But after another generation this same group of emerging college-and-seminary graduates had become more than half the whole number of ministers, and the only other large group was that of ministers who had graduated from seminary but had not been to college. Between these two types, the normal relation held: those who had more education averaged longer terms than those with less.

Of all the other educational groups that had included fairly large numbers in earlier years, none survived past 1830 in large numbers, and the only group of any significant size was that of the college graduates who had had no professional education. They numbered only twelve in 1860, a markedly older group, but with terms to date probably longer than could be accounted for by their age. As a matter of fact, the core of this small group were men settled in the smaller towns, living as enclaves little disturbed by the surrounding instability. Though raised in a period when seminary education was available, they continued a preseminary kind of education, with something of a preseminary permanence. In another half generation (that is, by 1875, the last year of Hazen's data), this group had dwindled away; except for a small, marginal group with no higher education at all, the only significant groups in the population were seminary graduates, the larger number of whom were college graduates, serving longer terms than those who had not been to college.

Some of these simple comparisons between educational types become confused if one isolates them according to tenure or the life history of the church, which is done in

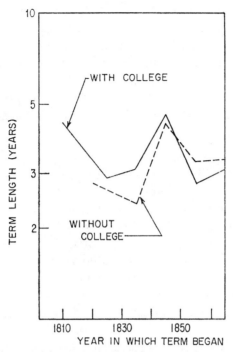

GRAPH 11. New Hampshire Congregational and Presbyterian clergy, average term lengths of ministers having some professional education and serving as supply. (*Source:* Hazen.)

Graphs 9-11. (Note that because some categories include too few terms for comparison in certain decades, they are not presented for those periods.) Some of the differences between educational types disappear. Other differences are reversed for certain decades. The reversals may sometimes reflect chance variation; that this is possible indicates that much of the broad difference in term lengths between educational groups resulted from the fact that the better-educated got more often into an institutional situation (settlement in a stable church) that carried some prospect for a longer term. For one decade, though, the reversal is itself a significant fact. In the 1840's, several groups enjoyed a distinct upturn in term lengths. This upturn showed for the whole ministerial population for the years 1839 to 1845, whether measured by terms ending in those years or by terms beginning in those years. Thus, terms were longer during the depression after the panics of 1837 and 1839. But the upturn does not show for all categories. The distinction is as follows:

Upturn in 1840's	*No upturn in 1840's*
Men with college but not professional education	College-and-seminary graduates
College graduates who attended seminary but did not graduate	Men who did private theological study, either with or without college
Seminary graduates without college	Men with no higher education
Men in unstable churches, with college and seminary education	Men in unstable churches, with professional education only
Men with no higher education, on supply	Men with no higher education, settled
Men in towns having a population of less than 1000 in 1870	Men in towns having a population of more than 9000 in 1870
Those on supply	Those installed
Those ordained	Those born in New Hampshire but outside the county where then serving

If this pattern meant simply that the kinds of men who usually had longer terms were less affected by short-term economic fluctuations, the phenomenon would not need explaining. Actually, the 1840 upturn gave to some of the men with mediocre "advantages" even longer terms than were then enjoyed by those with marked advantages of education, tenure, or location. There are three possible explanations, any or all of which may be valid. First, the depression may have produced in the lay population, or in persons who had been involved in the speculative, rapidly circulating pace of the 1830's, a reversion to old-time piety and hence a temporary disposition to retain ministers in the old-fashioned way. Second, the depression may have improved the *relative* ability of small towns and country areas to support ministers. Third, many ministers who had participated in the rapid circulation of the 1830's may have sought out small-town churches as places in which they could ride out the depression. The very sensitivity to economic advantage that would have made these men move from short term to short term in the thirties would have made them set even greater store than the average minister on having long terms in the early forties. This last explanation is the most plausible, as suggested by one rough statistical argument. The relative importance of town size as against career pattern in the upturn of the 1840's emerges if a separate series of average term lengths is constructed for each type of tenure within each major town-population group. (See Table 4.) It then appears that there was no consistent difference in pattern from one size of town to another, but that there was a fairly consistent difference in response between one kind of tenure and another. Ministers newly ordained furnish no clear-cut pattern: in some town groups they show the upturn in the 1840's; in other town groups they do not. After all, the "ordained pastor" label was attached to an early term in every man's career, even if it was only one that was to become a sequence of short stays. Once this initial term was

Table 4. Average term lengths (years) by decade term began, for selected decades, by form of tenure and 1870 population of town.

Decade, by first year	Ordained			Installed			Supply		
	0–999	1000–1999	2000 and over	0–999	1000–1999	2000 and over	0–999	1000–1999	2000 and over
1820	7.8	8.4	8.1	6.8	8.9	9.9	3.9	2.0	1.9
1830	7.4	9.1	3.2	8.2	7.0	7.8	2.9	2.9	2.4
1840	10.1	6.8	9.1	7.9	6.6	4.2	5.2	4.7	2.8
1850	8.1	5.3	8.5	6.0	6.8	4.7	2.9	3.2	2.3

Source: Hazen.

past, however, there was a plain difference between the men who were installed and those who served on supply. Those installed did not reflect the upturn of the 1840's in any of the three major population categories; those who served on supply showed the upturn in all of the population groups. It seems, therefore, that the upturn of the 1840's had more to do with individual attitudes than with the characteristics of particular places.

Much of any detailed argument about the 1840's must be speculative. One thing is not speculative—that ministers and congregations responded precisely to economic conditions. They adhered best to the old order when circumstances deprived them of the opportunity to behave expansively. Could the ministers who shared in this response have been sincere in complaining about the loss of permanency? Or did such ministers view permanency as a mere retreat from temporarily thwarted ambition? On this issue, was there any significant difference among the ministers themselves?

The age structure of the clergy gives a hint of just such a difference. Over the two centuries before 1875, certain regularities of age pattern characterized the group. The typical individual entered ministerial work at age twenty-six or twenty-seven in the eighteenth century, at about thirty in the nineteenth.[56] At any particular period, education made no difference in the age of ordination. Although migration into and out of New Hampshire may have affected the age distribution of the clergy from time to time, the largest shifts in that distribution resulted obviously from shifts in recruitment of young men into the profession. Immediately after any period in which a large number of men entered the body of available ministers, the ages of the whole group would be skewed downward for a time, then only gradually regain what appeared

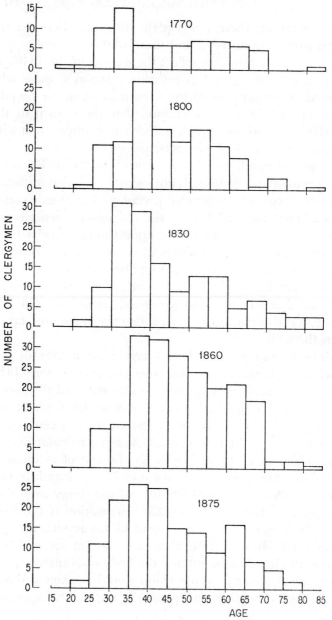

GRAPH 12. New Hampshire Congregational and Presbyterian clergy, age distribution for selected years, 1770-1875. (*Source:* Hazen.)

to be an underlying pattern. In this underlying pattern, a small fraction of the ministers working at any one time were in their twenties (not more than a tenth to an eighth of the whole number), about 30 per cent were in their thirties, and the proportion in each age decade after the thirties dropped off at a natural rate because of death. In the nineteenth century, nostalgic commentators sometimes thought that the ministers of the stable, earlier period had lived longer. This seems to have been a delusion. In 1800, for instance, the ministers were a distinctly more middle-aged group than in 1770.

Drastic shifts in age structure took place, however, between 1825 and 1875. (See Graph 12.) During the eighteenth century, recruitment into the clergy had progressed by well-defined stages, corresponding closely to stages in the settlement of New Hampshire, with minor shifts reflecting religious enthusiasm. (See Graph 13.) But no burst of enthusiasm brought so many ministers into the denomination as did the more institutionalized evangelizing that developed in the second quarter of the nineteenth century. New churches were being gathered in the state even then, but not nearly so fast as new ministers were being recruited, so that only through reduced permanency or migration from the state could the number of ministers and churches be brought into anything resembling equilibrium. This establishing of new churches, at a time when old churches were often weak, resulted in good part from denominational competition. After about 1815, groups as antipathetic as the Congregationalists and the Baptists used much the same language to describe the shortage of ministers in New England. Both lamented the number of "destitute" churches in the area—that is, the number of churches without a settled pastor—and both pointed to the number of towns in the north and west that

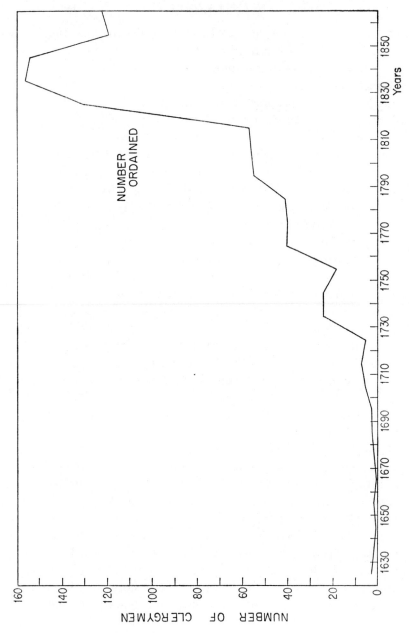

GRAPH 13. New Hampshire Congregational and Presbyterian clergy, number ordained in each decade. (*Source:* Hazen.)

had no gospel ministry at all. It was the Baptists who added to these points the complaint that what many towns lacked was the right *kind* of minister, the kind who would preach the genuine doctrines of the gospel. Presumably only decorum kept the Congregationalists from speaking in the same competitive tone. But for the New Hampshire Congregationalists, aggressive competition seems to have been limited to the second quarter of the century. At least after 1860, the absolute number of Congregationalist ministers in the state decreased, largely through a decrease in the number of active churches in the economically decadent country towns. As fewer ministers entered the profession, or at least as fewer entered who were available to serve in that state, the age structure of the group shifted back toward "normal." It had been markedly young just after the big influx of ministers; it was weighted heavily toward men in their late thirties or forties (relatively old for the typical minister) in the period when the ministers from this wave of recruitment began to enter middle age; it became mildly young again by 1875, when that generation of abnormal professional recruitment had largely disappeared from the active population.

This shifting age structure of the New Hampshire clergy raises two serious questions within the larger problem of explaining the collapse in permanency. Where did the influx of young men come from, and what kind of churches did they serve? The first of these questions does not, however, bring forth any significant information. In the groups for 1830 and 1860, the young men came typically from the seminaries and notably from the newer seminaries. That these schools were the channels for the recruitment drive of the period is no surprise. There seems, furthermore, to have been no great shift in the geographic origins of the clergy during the years when these men were becoming ministers, except that a slightly increased portion of the total had been born in New Hampshire. Here again, since New Hampshire was not a very attractive state to which to migrate, this shift is no surprise. But a classification according to the kinds of town in which the men served does produce a significant result. In the eighteenth century, the age of ministers differed little between the small towns and the largest ones. As late as 1800, there was still no significant difference in the age structures of clergy in small and large towns. From 1830 on, there was a difference. The larger towns had consistently younger ministers than the smaller ones. Specifically, only a small fraction of ministers in the large towns were even as old as the average age for the whole population of ministers. (See Graph 14 and Table 5.) Since the large towns had a higher proportion of "stable" churches, and since they had larger congregations with more money, they could presumably get the kind of men they preferred. And they preferred young men— young not just in the sense of "in their prime," young not in the sense of being in their forties or fifties, but young meaning in their thirties, not having yet reached an age of "gravity" relative to the ages of the strong laymen of the congregations. This preference confirms what might otherwise appear to be one of the most subjective, biased complaints that ministers made during the middle years of the nineteenth century: that churches in looking for new ministers preferred, not the man of maturity and profundity, but the novelty, the fresh personality, and—often the specific complaint—the young man. This fact raises many questions about the nature of American society in that period, questions hardly to be answered by a statistical study of the ministers of one denomination in one state. It raises especially the question of whether the democracy of midcentury preferred superficial values and mere novelty as such.

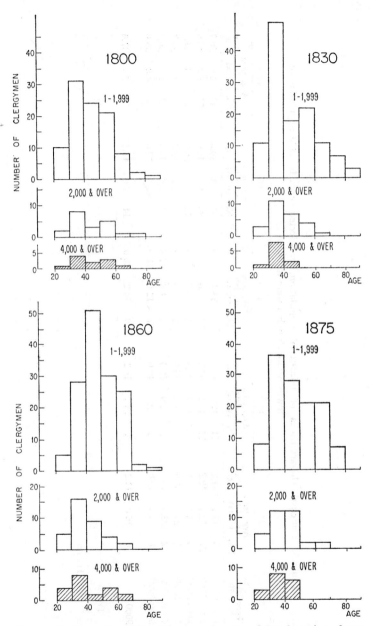

GRAPH 14. New Hampshire Congregational and Presbyterian clergy, age distribution for selected years, 1800-1875, broken down by the 1870 population of towns where ministers were serving. (*Source:* Hazen.)

Table 5. Principal characteristics of ministerial population, for selected years, by 1870 population of towns where churches were located.

Population in 1870	1770			1800			1830			1860			1875		
	No.	Avg. term to date (years)	Avg. age	No.	Avg. term to date (years)	Avg. age	No.	Avg. term to date (years)	Avg. age	No.	Avg. term to date (years)	Avg. age	No.	Avg. term to date (years)	Avg. age
0-999	26	17.4	44.2	41	12.5	46.0	49	13.1	48.3	55	7.1	49.6	47	5.6	50.7
1000-1999	31	12.4	42.2	57	14.1	45.5	72	12.6	45.3	89	7.1	49.6	74	3.7	46.0
2000-2999	5	5.4	39.2	7	12.7	42.8	11	8.7	46.5	12	6.4	39.8	13	4.9	41.6
3000-3999	2	24.5	57.5	2	19.0	46.5	3	5.0	42.7	5	5.2	43.6	3	4.0	50.7
4000-4999	2	22.0	50.0	3	12.0	40.3	4	1.8	31.8	4	7.0	41.3	3	2.0	36.0
5000-5999	1	9.0	39.0	1	22.0	49.0	1	12.0	40.0	1	42.0	70.0	2	4.0	36.0
9000 +	6	16.0	43.2	7	18.4	48.3	6	8.2	36.0	14	9.6	41.4	12	3.9	37.6
Totals	73			118			146			180			154		

Source: Hazen.

The data on the New Hampshire Congregational clergy show the growth of a differentiated labor market among what had been a fairly homogeneous profession, a market within which (quite aside from any issue of westward migration) there existed routine channels for the movement of individuals from one segment to another. There were three main segments: the country towns, among which the majority of ministers circulated throughout their whole careers; the medium-sized cities, which included all the largest towns in New Hampshire, and which as a group siphoned off the preferred among the younger ministers; and the metropolitan cities, which in New England included Boston, Hartford, and Providence.

In 1830, when the Unitarian upset was still recent, the age of orthodox ministers in Boston averaged about thirty-nine, and they had been in office on the average only about four years. They were thus almost as young as those in the large New Hampshire towns (although they were older than the Unitarian ministers in Boston), and had been in office for an even shorter time.[57] But by the 1870's, the Boston ministers were at least as old as those in the smallest towns in New Hampshire, yet had been in office twice as long as the New Hampshire ministers.[58] They had, in fact, been in office for about ten years, on the average—that is, for almost the same number of years as the difference in age between them and the ministers in the large New Hampshire towns. While there may be some hidden explanation for this pattern, the only obvious explanation is that the metropolis was drawing its ministers from those large towns that had already selected the preferred among the young men, and that the metropolis then became the only segment within the ministerial labor market that not only had the men it really wanted but could give them long terms.

The fragmentation of ministerial careers made real and more complex a separation of career lines into different "tracks" that had only begun to appear in the days of permanency. Earlier, ministers had occasionally left a small-town church for a better position in a city. They had rarely felt much temptation to go to centers of lesser grade than Boston, however, and they had not moved in sufficient numbers to affect the way fellows in the profession would perceive their own chances. Now, by the middle years of the nineteenth century, those who began their careers in small-town churches found that they had a limited future. Few even preached more than a few years in any one town. Few even got churches in large towns or cities. They could expect only to wander disjointedly from one village to another, repeatedly entering the situation that sentimental myth praised for its rootedness, yet rarely staying long enough to add their own roots to the local pattern. The men who began preaching in the larger towns or cities had access to a more attractive, even if less certain, future. These were the men who were visible when churches in Portland, Hartford, Brooklyn, or even Boston took New Hampshire within the sphere where they looked for promising young men. These were the men who turned up occasionally as seminary professors or as secretaries to church mission boards. These men, too, sometimes found in their large-town churches a permanency of tenure that almost never fell to the small-town preacher.

Their fortunes varied, of course. Some, who began in marginal or mission churches in towns like Manchester, had chances no better than men in small-town churches. Some simply failed, and either accepted a series of short-term charges in minor churches, or moved out of the ministry into other professions or into obscurity. Those who reached a large-town church only toward the middle of their lives generally continued to operate in the large-town circuit. But those who got to the large-town circuit while they were still in their thirties stood a fair chance of moving on to public careers in city churches or in the religious bureaucracy.[59] This whole pattern could only mean the growth of "social distance" inside the profession. Men on one track could know, even if disjointedly, the world of country life; increasingly, they would become intellectual commodities, shunted from place to place as country people sought to bring in new talent who would either maintain contact with the outside world or offer some validation to rural isolation. These ministers themselves could only learn how real was such isolation and how artificial was any outside contact that they offered. Those men who had moved into the outside world would, on the other hand, have real access to the intellectual life of Congregationalism, some real share in the social life of the larger nation—and an increasingly abstract, schematic, condescending view of how the bulk of their profession operated. This could only add to any intellectual tensions within the profession, putting a premium on the work of church bureaucrats who could mediate blandly between the unmeeting strata.

The Underlying Causes of Decline

Statistical analysis tells less why than how and when permanency declined. The reasons emerge from the histories of individual churches. Of course, even among those New Hampshire churches that showed the decline in permanency at the same time as the "average" church, some were special cases. Some went through a change of denomination, dropping abruptly the minister of the rejected doctrine. Others were in the process of decay as organizations, and became defunct early in the nineteenth century.

While this decay may sometimes have resulted from doctrinal secession or disaffection, it probably meant just as often that the towns in question had never had the economic strength to maintain a secure religious organization with a paid leader.[60]

But these gross faults in the life histories of particular churches beg the question of why permanency declined. Although only a small proportion of churches showed such faults in any obvious way, nearly all New Hampshire churches were affected by the phenomenon of decline. On the other hand, a doctrinal quarrel could break off one pastorate without ending the practice of long-term pastorates in the church involved. In 1817 David Oliphant was forced out of Keene, where he had come only three years earlier, because of a quarrel between the "liberal" town and the "narrow" church members;[61] but the Congregational church there then settled Zedekiah Barstow, who stayed until he died in 1873.

But nearly a fifth of the churches felt the decline in "pure" form: the break in length hit terms that began sometime between 1790 and 1820, and the life histories of the churches show no glaring fault that can serve as ready-made explanation. The records and local histories of these churches, as they merge into pattern, are the flesh that can explain motion in the statistical skeleton.[62]

Often the official explanations of why a pastorate ended short of the proper term yield little explanatory sense. Chester Colton left Brentwood in 1825, supposedly on his own initiative, because an eye disease kept him from studying.[63] But in many particular cases there is no evidence whether disease excuses were physiologically honest, psychosomatic, or simply lying[64] covers for other reasons. Unless a dismission for health reasons actually indicates ulterior motives, such a case leaves serious explanation to be sought elsewhere.

The elements of an explicit pattern were visible in New England well before the main period of decline, as in the quarrel between Eleazar Wheelock and the people of the North Parish in Lebanon, Connecticut, just before he left the ministry to become president of Dartmouth College in 1770. Wheelock had been pastor in Lebanon North for over thirty years. He had quarreled often with his people, but neither he nor they had seemed to consider the quarreling alone a reason to break the relation. As Wheelock began to work out with backers a plan for converting his Indian charity school into a real college he felt coerced toward a break by other difficulties. He complained about his health, insisting that he could no longer handle regular pastoral duties, insisting too that he needed the school as a situation that would permit him to be useful in retirement. He could not make his complaints about his salary more specific than he long had, but he now stated them in a form that sounded like a final summary after years of trouble. He accused the people of ignoring the services of the gospel; this, he said, and not any vices or any economic handicap, was the cause for their not prospering in this world the way neighboring communities did. He argued, to put it in crude terms, that they had not primed the gospel pump and were therefore being punished for their niggardliness. In 1766, he asked the church to consider calling another man to preach on trial, and he promised to agree to his own dismission as soon as a new man was settled.[65] Then his assumptions went bad. When his backers in England failed to come through with a definite college plan as early as Wheelock had expected, he was in danger of having no place to go, since the church had asked a new man to come on trial, and since the town had moved to dissolve Wheelock's civil contract without waiting for a formal dismission. He quickly announced that his health had improved, and that he wanted to stay over the winter, until news came from England. He reminded the people of his stipulation that they should actually settle a new man before he would himself leave. In the end the town persisted, Wheelock procrastinated, and the affair dragged on until a new season brought favorable news from England.[66]

The crucial elements in this story are the environment— that is, a local community trying to operate on a thin economic base—and the rise of conflicting impulses toward improving the situation. The parties to church problems knew that economic progress might solve many problems, creating a margin within which the people could support a ministry without anxious calculation. But the whole New England back country tended from the late eighteenth century to become like Wheelock's Lebanon: a region suffering from poverty while other areas developed increasing competitive advantages.

In its effects on the prosperity of the orthodox churches, the way men fought decline only tightened conflict. Some men sought to raise their own status, acquiring a social and intellectual urbanity that would serve as values while society lost the resources to support value. This individual impulse had old roots in the differentiation of a commercial order from the rest of New England, and found a continuing outlet in various moves toward theological rationalism. Where people wanted their minister to symbolize gentility as well as social unity, they encouraged this impulse in him. It contributed to the Unitarian split, and its apparent growth even before the end of the eighteenth century may have stimulated some of the countersecession by Methodists, Baptists, and Universalists whom urbanity alienated.

Other men, including some who remained in the orthodox communion, sought improvement through building new organizations: colleges, seminaries, benevolent societies. This required them to secede from particular parishes in order to become presidents or professors or secretaries, it brought into question the sincerity of their allegiance to the New England pastorate as an institution, and it created salary envies between pastors and bureaucrats.[67] Wheellock's defensiveness, stated even while he consummated the act of desertion, provided an early model for such ministerial behavior.

Not all the impulses to improvement revealed arguable motives in the minister himself. Many people, ministers included, accepted the fact of local economic decline and moved west. Resettlement had a firm place in the Congregational tradition. When it resulted in the organization of new churches, which supported pastors, it did no ideological violence to the system; and, except for the serious matter that it meant a desertion of "home," it did no emotional violence. What it really did was demographic violence; it drew off inhabitants who might have contributed their mites to support pastors. It thus had the same effect as did those denominational secessions that gave expression to social cleavage.

Finally, improvement took the form of urbanization. As in many parts of the country, this meant not only the growth of real cities, but the drive to make each village into a separate, competing entity, perhaps cherishing the fantasy of ultimate growth to dominance, and meanwhile struggling to support its own social apparatus, including a church house to "facilitate its progress."[68] While genuine urbanization drew population to the metropolis and the factory, internal migration and secession had a corrosive effect on existing communities, much as did westward migration and denominational splits.

Impulses toward personal and local improvement tended to fragment local society, while its economic strength was declining anyway. This culminating desertion of stability had repeated effects on the pastoral relation. The tempo of money quarrels increased. While plain loss of prosperity was the underlying cause, occasions to quarrel came from discontinuities in the economic system: from inflation as such, from changes to a new kind of currency in the years after the Revolution, and from shifts in the balance between value of money and value of produce. This last problem, just as in the earlier Parsons' Cause in Virginia, gave churches an opportunity to play sharp tricks on ministers, adapting the form of payment to whatever would save the parish money at a particular time.[69] Such quarrels bore especially on the welfare features of the old pastoral relation. People who had trouble selling crops and had to share group burdens among a smaller number of persons because neighbors left for sectarianism or the West, did not like to pay double salaries, one to an infirm pastor and one to an active colleague. More and more after 1820, the elderly minister lived in retirement, without organizational ties except as member of some church. When a church council in New Ipswich, New Hampshire, advised in 1860 that the church there grant an annuity to the retiring Samuel Lee, it did argue that the church had a moral obligation to its pastor, who was infirm at the age of fifty-seven; but this council paid more attention to the fact that Lee's resignation was necessary if a seceding group was to rejoin the church. The annuity, in other words, was intended to buy Lee off, and hardly represented much continuity with tradition.[70]

Doctrinal quarrels were at work in some breaks in permanency, even where the church itself remained intact.[71] Such quarrels, overt or covert, also put strains on the minor welfare features of the pastoral relation. Besides threatening parsonage houses and lands, they broke up or reduced the circles of cooperating neighboring ministers. Exchanging of pulpits became less easy, cutting into a form of variety or vacation that the pastor had enjoyed; and the prospective minister began to insist that his contract allow him three or four Sundays a year off to "visit my distant friends."[72] Pallbearers' preaching as a benefit for the widow became an antiquity, a merely remembered custom. Denominational splits also brought the weakening and eventual abandonment of the legal requirement that towns support an orthodox minister. While the withdrawal of legal coercion had little direct effect on permanency, denominational competition over declining resources probably had much, in the same way that the splitting and multiplying of towns reduced support.

The tendency to localism that defined the locality in narrow terms also brought shifts in what a minister meant to church unity. Localism often meant lay control, perhaps by the unconverted members of parish or town, perhaps by the deacons and other strong members of the church itself. While an older usage had embraced both pastoral authority and congregational discipline as techniques for preserving unity, a split between these forms now appeared.[73] The church in Durham is an example of what happened. There, in a town that had long been poor, the Congregationalist church was struggling against Baptist and Christian Church secessions. In 1780, when it settled a minister, it did adopt a confession of faith that put strong emphasis on the obligation of the church to support a pastor and on the responsibility of pastors as elders. Then in 1793, while the same man was still pastor, the church adopted a new confession and covenant. Besides dropping the old Cambridge Platform, which had spelled out basic features of New England polity, on the ground that few people had copies of it, the church put in place of the 1780 pastoral responsibility clause a statement that "Christians are bound to maintain a course of gospel discipline and holy watchfulness, over one another, agreeably to the directions given by inspiration, that Christ may be honoured in his house, and glorified before the world." A little later, when this church had only some seven members, and went for eleven years without a pastor, the members remained active as a church meeting, using the techniques of church discipline to keep watch on their group life.[74] At New Ipswich, a similar town, the strong-willed Samuel Lee interpreted the tensions leading to his dismission as the result of long uncertainty in the church between two kinds of control: that by a pastor who would lead and not fear some dissent, and that by a lay leadership willing to make excessive use of formal discipline, bringing even their pastor himself to account.[75] In the churches there thus grew a tension between an outward conception of unity, projecting difficulties through the pastor into the larger world, and an inward conception, concerning itself with the detailed acts of unity or disunity between one member and another. The latter was appropriate in a community whose poverty or decline threw its remaining members close upon each other. It gave ideological texture to what would otherwise have been the crass breaking of business relations between church and minister.

Ministers, too, could redefine situations while seeming to accept unpleasant facts in a spirit of propriety. Nathan Lord, in Amherst, New Hampshire, recognized the forces that weakened the community he served, and agreed to accept a cut of $100 from his $850 salary. But he made his acceptance conditional upon both the welfare of the local church and on the ability of his family to continue subsisting on the smaller amount.[76] He thus succeeded in injecting a conditional element into a contract that had traditionally been open to cancellation only by mutual consent. This implicit bargain was about as far as the erosion of the pastorate could go by merely implicit means; in fact, creation of a new explicit system had already begun.

Although some generalization was explicit in the idea, circulating about 1826, that a "people should have a new minister once in ten years."[77] the psychological core of the new system was the hardening of hearts that worked in churches as they realized that they could rid themselves even of aged ministers, and in ministers as they realized that a few words about seeking "a greater sphere of usefulness" would cover any careerist move. The techniques of the new system were two: a new kind of ministerial contract, and a diffusely rationalized program of ministerial recruitment.

New contracts appeared in New Hampshire as early as 1795. Typically, they specified that a man would supply a church's pulpit for two to five years, after which either party might cancel the connection with proper notice. Sometimes, contracts omitted any definite term, allowing cancellation at any time on, say, six months' notice. Church councils may not have liked to admit that such a contract provided in itself the adequate basis for leaving a church, but they did notice the practice and go along with it.[78]

The new recruitment system, operating through the societies for subsidizing the education of young men in the ministry, came to terms with the facts that American population was growing faster than the supply of "orthodox" preachers and that secular professions had been growing faster than the clerical. Population trends in rural New England, however, threw such calculations askew. It was one thing to seek additional men for the Northwest, where vigorous new communities had no indigenous ministers. It was another to seek them for an area where churches had been dying, where towns had been ceasing to support the gospel, and where whole populations had become too poor to pay salaries that would retain pastors. Yet men like Francis Brown, the president of Dartmouth in 1818, insisted on the "strenuous use of all appointed means for augmenting the number of qualified teachers of religion," and especially for supplying destitute "spots, which have been rendered sacred by the visitations of the Holy Spirit since the first settlement of the country."[79] If, up to a point, this was just the standard effort to fight erosion by ignoring it, throwing new material where it would be washed away in the old gullying, Brown yet implied a need for the particular kind of men who would be willing to go into the destitute parishes. Probably, out of politeness to future recruits, he did not spell out what this meant: that to fill up the spaces men would have to be found who would accept insecurity and low incomes, either as a lifelong way of living, or as an introduction into the clergy.

This need, combined with the growing indifference to the security of old pastors,[80] meant that in the absence of other influences a three-stage ministerial career became the pattern for lives that had once assumed a single, lifelong pastorate. The minister who fitted the pattern would begin with a term at a church that could no longer afford a real pastor, would then spend a term of his mature years at a stronger church, and would finally spend some years either in retirement or in again supplying pulpits of weak churches.[81] This three-part fragmentation alone would have accounted for the greater part of the arithmetic decline in permanency. The inability or unwillingness of the people to support ministers was one part of this picture. But another was an evangelical denomination's determination to retain contact with all areas where it had ever been planted. This determination tended to force the social status of ministers downward.

In this effect the chain of local pressures operating in New Hampshire came to the outcome shown by statistical data on the age structure of the ministry. Similarly, the way that ministers and laymen alike talked about their desires to promote personal usefulness or civic pride constituted much the same sensitivity to economic opportunity that emerges from data on the ministerial terms of the 1840's. Two factors operated in the collapse of permanency: the relative economic decline of rural areas, and the initiatives men took to create new, self-protective values at the expense of, or as a replacement for, older communal ones.

RESPONSES TO IMPERMANENCY, 1835-1886

Hazen's data, combined with selected data from other collections, rule out certain overly simple explanations for the collapse in permanency; they outline the development of an increasingly segmented, articulated labor market; and they show that none of the supposed advantages that accrued to one kind of minister or another made nearly so much difference as the historical event of the collapse in permanency. Even the deep difference in length of term between men installed and men serving on supply became a minor one after 1830. Professional education, which continued to confer mild advantage after 1830, meant terms no more than a fraction as long as the generation-long settlements of the eighteenth century. No obvious method of regaining permanency was open to the

ministers. Some men spoke realistically about how to regain wholly lost ground, as when a preacher at an 1817
ordination in Durham urged the need for Christians in
destitute places to do everything possible for union among
themselves in order to maintain a pious and learned
ministry.[82] But regaining the length of terms, in places that
did support ministers, was a less hopeful task.

It did not suffice to respond to impermanence by accepting it, as by adopting its contractual forms. Without
some sense of security, men in the New England churches
felt a painful break with their tradition. Daniel Dana's was
only the worst case: When he left the First Presbyterian
Church in Newburyport in 1820 to become president of
Dartmouth, he had a breakdown that forced him to resign
from Dartmouth in little over a year. After floundering
through a short term as minister of a Presbyterian church
in Londonderry, New Hampshire, for five years, he returned to the "small" Second Presbyterian Church in
Newburyport, where he could serve in his declining years.
Throughout the latter part of his life, the shock and guilt
of the self-imposed break from the First Church kept returning as a burden in his discourse.[83]

Real adjustment to new conditions took several forms,
two of which showed locally before they did nationally.
First, existing bodies of ministers had to decide what to do
with ministers who were not pastors. The Hopkinton Association in New Hampshire had long encouraged candidates, licentiates, and visiting ministers to sit in on its
meetings. Now, in 1837, it debated whether to accept as
full members men who did not have a regular pastoral
charge. Characteristically, since the adjustment was just beginning, it postponed any formal decision, but after about
1840 it began to accept such members.[84] Second, individual
ministers faced a conflict between the moves that circum-

stances demanded and the stability that tradition required. The churches had for years been ordaining men at large to go out as missionaries, but this practice did not quite meet the general problem. Charles Walker, pastor in New Ipswich, faced up to it in 1835. A conscientious man, he felt that he should leave his church because a small minority was dissatisfied with him. Persisting in this feeling even when a church committee asked him to stay, he argued that the "frequent exchange of ministers, so common at the present day, was thought to be a great evil, one that encourages a spirit of dissatisfaction and disunion on very slight grounds; that injures the usefulness of many ministers, and undermines the foundations of society." He then tried to find general principles on which to justify his departure, when most of his church stood by the ideal of permanency. The point he found and stressed was this: "Ministers are the property of the church at large."[85] The breakdown of local community could be forgotten if only men would define the "real" community as something wider and more complex.

The evolution to a national acceptance of Walker's insight was not easy, and the resistance to it had creative results. The apparent futility of the situation made realistic one sentimental feature in many discussions of permanency: their repeated insistence that what permanency really required was a change of "spirit" among congregations and ministers alike. Ministers went through the form of arguing that a change of spirit would result in an actual lengthening of terms.[86] What they were actually saying was that, since no practical course could improve matters much, people might as well make the best of the situation by finding new meanings that they could impute to the minister's position. As the search for new meanings tapped the historical thinking of the period, clergymen developed an increasingly precise sense of what their status had been in the past. Often they warped that historical sense to support some useful myth, but they produced some substantial scholarship. Men became newly self-conscious about the Congregational way or the New England way, and men like Henry Martyn Dexter argued persuasively that permanency was an essential part of that way as it had developed by the late seventeenth century. Through their expositions of the Congregational past, they argued that the settled pastor ordained by a local church was the only real minister, that stated supplies were a modern abuse, and that the ordination of evangelists was an infection from prelacy.[87] But they achieved their historical consciousness through a thoroughly academic, "nineteenth-century" scholarship. Technical in mind and style, these church historians lived according to a high-toned professionalism that they opposed in their writing.

Other, more practical men defended professionalism. From about 1840 on, much of the leadership within the Congregational churches began to repudiate the old definitions of the ministry in terms of membership in an organic community. They defined it rather in terms of the minister's occupation as such: a rank or label that he could carry from community to community, retaining it even if he were attached to no local church at all. Edwards A. Park, of the Andover Theological Seminary, stated this idea to the Pastoral Association of Massachusetts in 1844; the ministers then proposed it for adoption into the scheme of Congregational polity. Park wanted the clergy to accept professionalism and the mass society through a single strategy: let ministers accept the fact that they were an order set permanently apart from the laity, an order whose competent concern for theology they could not communicate to the mass; let them derive their standing and their prestige from each other, dispensing a popular product to the populace and reserving abstruse theological discussion for their private meetings. Park's view smacked of the prudent crypto-whiggery that observers noted in his generation: the tendency for self-consciously select groups to build ways of life sheltered from the democratic glare. While warning the ministers "to be circumspect in their treatment of the laity," he believed that their learned concerns

should *distinguish* them from those whom they instruct, should help to make them "a chosen generation," " a peculiar" class, "a royal priesthood." And before we confound all distinction in this regard, between the minister and the layman, before we make the mass of the people umpires in strictly metaphysical disputes, before we abandon all parts of theological science which are not congenial with the popular taste, we do well to be circumspect. We should remember that in our land the clergymen who are supported by the people, must in a measure supply the place of the professed theologians in Europe, who are supported by the State; must be the guardians and standard-bearers of truth; must attempt the rare union of a studious habit with practical wisdom.[88]

As an Anglo-Catholic pamphleteer pointed out, Park's conception of the ministry as a separate, permanent order made sense in terms of any honestly hierarchical church, but it did not quite become Congregationalism, especially not if presented in an address that included, as Park's did, some standard gibes at Catholicism.[89]

The Congregationalist ministers whom Park addressed did not seem properly embarrassed by any inconsistency. They produced a committee to revise the Cambridge Platform, and the committee managed to bridge old and new through careful evasion. The seventeenth-century statement of Congregational polity had recognized as ministers only those men who currently held office as pastors of particular churches; it did not accord the status to men who had left one charge but had not yet been installed to another, and it made no exceptions. In form, the committee of 1844 defended this general principle; but it accepted particular exceptions that made a difference: "It is not according to sound ecclesiastical principles, nor would it tend to promote the interests of religion, for any men, except those who are destined to the missionary service, or those who hold special offices in colleges or theological seminaries, to be ordained at large, or, without particular pastoral charge." And in its statements on discipline the committee included the "settled principle, that every Congregational minister, is really under the watch and care of the Congregational denomination, and that no one can evade this inspection by neglecting to unite himself with an association, or by refusing to acknowledge that he is, under God, responsible to his brethren, and liable to be called to account by them for heresy or immorality."[90] The 1840's, however, were a bit early for even this cautious high-toned approach. The committee proposals, much as they may have represented the trend of Congregationalism, met no better response than had Cotton Mather's Boston Proposals of 140 years earlier.

Not until 1865 did something like this revision go through. In the 1840's and 1850's the Congregationalists finally accepted the fact that their earlier cooperation with the Presbyterians in the home missions field was not going to work, and they began to push more vigorously into the Middle West as an identifiable denomination. The older New England concept of the church and of the pastoral relation did not fit well the needs of communities where other denominations were already established, and where the Congregationalists had in their favor no assumption that they were the one normal religious persuasion. Needing other techniques, those on the scene often adapted their traditional practice to the demands of the situation or to the example of their competitors. This created an embarrassment within the whole communion. All felt compelled to acknowledge the New England standard, yet the Midwesterners had begun to adopt more of the by then ordinary denominational pattern. The Midwesterners thought they needed to continue further in this new direction, and they wanted to get the sanction of the whole persuasion.

Possibly they and the New Englanders might have delayed indefinitely facing this embarrassing divergence in practice, had not the conclusion of the Civil War cut through difficulties, offering the usual post war chance to construct a better world. Congregationalists now had the opportunity, they told themselves, to evangelize the freedmen and the poor whites of the South. Specifically to meet this need, and incidentally to discuss and renew almost every other topic of common interest, they held a grand National Council in Boston in 1865. In a special resolution, this council lumped together the problems of Western and Southern evangelization, recognizing the needs to find quickly the necessary preachers, to accept them even without the proper education, and to accept even lay preachers. This adjustment in ideas on the ministry was disguised by obeisance to the educational ideal, and it was on the surface confined to the work in newly opened areas, but it was made.[91]

At the same time the Council adopted a general (but of course unauthoritative) description of Congregational polity. For the first time in the history of Congregational platforms, this description included a special section on the ministry rather than treating it as an element within the local church, and it defined as ministers all those who had ever been ordained or recognized by a proper church group, whether or not they were working with any particular local church or had ever worked with a local church.[92] Leonard Bacon, who had helped draft the new platform and who then had the task of expounding it on the floor of the Council, said that one of its main points was the recognition of a

professional ministry, consisting of men devoted and consecrated by ordination to the work of preaching the gospel. That is not in the Cambridge Platform. It was not really in the theory of the founders of the New England churches, for they did not see, in all respects, the working and application of their own principles. They held to lay preaching—what they called "prophesying,"—but they did not see how to recognize any man as a minister of the gospel who was not an officer of the church.

.   .   .   .   .

We have outgrown that, and it is an inevitable necessity for us to outgrow it. We have none of the fear which they had, that a ministry would be a hierarchy. Our churches have grown to age, and can take care of themselves.[93]

What had been stated covertly in 1844 could be explained frankly and informally in 1865, and there was in fact little argument on the floor over the section of the platform dealing with the ministry. The shift in definition was finally recognized: orientation to the community had been replaced by orientation to the clerical profession and to the denomination.

During the twenty years after the decision of 1865, Congregationalists continued to tug back and forth over the definition of the new outlook. The discussion centered sometimes on education, sometimes on the distinction between settled pastors and stated supplies, sometimes on the parish system whereby influential members of a congregation who were not church members could influence the hiring and firing of ministers. In 1880, controversy centered on permanency as such, and at all times permanency tended to enter into other discussions as a criterion of virtue. The 1880 discussion was in fact the most objective treatment of the subject produced by any person or group from the time that the concern for permanency had begun. A committee conducted an elaborate correspondence with people who presumably knew the reasons for particular breaks in ministers' terms, and it made a statistical breakdown of term lengths according to the number of members in each church. From its correspondence it got much the same explanation for impermanence that ministers had been offering for a generation or more, with the addition that many blamed the parish system for interfering with terms. From its statistical work it got a significant result: that the churches with vacant ministries or with short terms were concentrated among those that had small memberships. The committee had nothing to make of its investigation, though, and came up with the same recommendation for a "better mind in the churches" that had characterized many earlier discussions.[94]

Nor did any of the other controversies on ministerial status come to a definite conclusion. The nearest thing to a resolution during those years was a decision by the American College and Education Society to concentrate its financial aid on students who were committed to the full college plus seminary course; while making some exceptions, it repudiated the loosening of educational standards that had followed the Civil War.[95] This seemed a victory for New England against the Middle West, yet the old regional tensions continued, and interlocked with similar tensions within New England. It was Midwesterners who insisted that church statistics should drop what they considered an invidious distinction between pastors and "acting pastors" (the euphemism that had been adopted in place of the older term "stated supplies"). It was the secretary of the National Council, a New Englander, who insisted on this distinction and who also put a great stress on permanency in his reports.[96] Within New England, the tension lay between purists like Henry Martyn Dexter who attacked the parish system, and leading pastors like Nathaniel Bouton of Concord, New Hampshire, who defended the system as the only way the churches could get precisely that financial support necessary to give ministers long terms.[97]

Although there were some inconsistencies of pattern, the "practical" men of New England seemed to sympathize with the Midwesterners much of the time. Bouton, for instance, had in 1865 been the man who moved the final adoption of the report on evangelization in the West and the South.[98] Because Congregational polity was loose, the National Council did not have to make a decision on any of these issues except the trifling one of the designations to be given different kinds of ministers in its statistical reports. There it dropped the offensive "acting pastor" but added a new abbreviation, "P.C.," to designate those pastors who were installed by councils.[99] This symbolized the way into which Congregationalists settled by the 1880's: the purists were allowed to keep some positive sign of the values, and all parties continued to pay lip service to the ideal of permanency, but the practical men and the Midwesterners served notice that they would suffer no censure from tradition.

Over the nineteenth century, the Congregational ministry became no less of an "office-holding" profession than it had been in the eighteenth century. Individual ministers became, if anything, even less involved than they had been before in the day to day transactions of the market. Only the itinerant evangelists who never found much welcome among Congregationalists came anywhere near the pattern of a fee-for-service profession. By resisting this extreme version of market orientation even during the momentum of the collapse in permanency, Congregationalists preserved a continuity between the communal office holding of the eighteenth century and the organizational, stratified office holding of the middle and late nineteenth century. The period of collapse was a gap that the ministers could tense over only through expedients—at times through a retrospection that was rarely real history, at times through a crypto-whiggery that soon ceased to be real conservatism. But the continuity was preserved, and the expedients may have been the normal price paid for order.

V

Stasis, 1850

Talk about "excellence" titillates Americans. It also disturbs them, because it seems to endanger equality in a society that has all the resources and the complexity to nurture great inequality. At least in the past, it has also set Americans to thinking about the professions. For this association of ideas there are perhaps two reasons. First, men could relegate the task of pursuing high standards to certain groups, giving the professional the job of doing well, and thus insulating the bulk of society from the threat of inequality. Second, people realized, with varying degrees of sophistication, that the groups conventionally labeled professions had been largely responsible for any drive toward excellence in this country.

These groups have not always tried equally hard to promote achievement. True, for a generation or so, beginning about 1750, men in each of the learned professions tried to raise both the intellectual level and the practical performance of their groups. They knew that the professions had been adequate, but no more than adequate, to the needs of a semideveloped colony. There had been no professional schools in British America, and virtually no bodies devoted to licensure or professional discipline. Apprenticeship there was, to a lawyer or a doctor or a minister. Informal controls there were, sometimes exercised by clubs of fellows within a calling. Groups devoted to the advancement of knowledge there were, but these often took so much of knowledge for their province that they could do little for any specialized segment of it. For anything

more ambitious, men looked to the Inns of Court in England, they looked to the hospitals and medical schools of
London or Edinburgh; they looked to a classis in Holland,
a bishop in London, or even to a Wesley. As they looked,
they saw how vulnerable the transoceanic dependence was.
There was one serious exception to the pattern of provincial mediocrity, in the success with which Puritan or
Calvinist intellectual standards had migrated to the New
World, but not everyone would claim that Puritan clerical
performance retained in 1750 either the fire or the precision it had displayed a century earlier.

Soon after midcentury, men began efforts to sharpen,
raise, and institutionalize professional status within the
groups affected. Medical students exposed to British conditions returned to America feeling a drive to establish
schools and hospitals in their own cities. In the case of
Samuel Bard, for instance, it is easy to see how the student
in Edinburgh began to worry about finding a place for
himself in the medical profession back in New York; how
Bard's father, who was also a physician, but one practicing
without a medical degree on the basis of an ordinary apprenticeship, warned the son that excessive personal ambition would only defeat itself; and how the son then
sank his private ambition in an effort to organize (and of
course to benefit from) group projects like a hospital and
a medical school for the city of New York.[1]

Sometimes the sharpening of status took superficial form,
as in one effort to introduce a distinctive hair style for
surgeons,[2] or in more successful efforts to introduce gowns
and wigs for the legal profession.[3] Sometimes it took on
high seriousness, as in the ambitious system building that
divines or legal commentators or physicians undertook during the last decades of the eighteenth century and into the
early years of the nineteenth. Sometimes the efforts toward

status became controversial, as in the proposals to give
American Anglicans their own bishop. But whether these
efforts dealt with symbols, organization, or the substance of
professional training and knowledge, they began well before the Revolution and lasted until well afterward, uniting impulses toward hierarchy with superficially different
impulses toward giving America its own panoply of social
institutions.

If one looks from this picture to the prospect about 1850,
the professions suddenly appear headed in the opposite direction, recoiling before great Jacksonian attacks on aristocracy and privilege, falling in with a democratic trend
toward conformity—or toward an individualism that somehow assumed that all individuals were alike. The learned
professions were retreating toward mediocrity. Not all in
the same way, of course: the clergy in Massachusetts did
not necessarily move on the same track as the medical profession of New York. But certain incidents of the 1840's
seemed to point up the similarities underlying the natural
variety of response.

Consider first how the bar fared at the New York
state consitutional convention of 1846.[4] Several "emergen-
cies"[5] led to this convention, among them a political demand that the people elect officials directly, and a complaint that the court system had become inefficient and
remote. The convention did make judges elective. It also
debated the work of practicing lawyers in connection with
three different subjects.

Proponents of legal codification discussed abuses in practice as one reason why the convention should instruct the
legislature to adopt simplified codes. Certain groups wanted
to circumvent "real" lawyers altogether by increasing the
competence of justices of the peace, or by establishing
courts of conciliation. In a very rough way, these moves

seemed to show city merchants acting with western New York farmers against the lawyers and the Irish.[6] A distinction appeared, though, between the arguments used by a dogged, ambitious courtroom lawyer like Charles O'Conor and the ideas advanced by established commercial lawyers. O'Conor, an immigrant who had struggled up to eminence at the traditional forensic bar, fought any proposals to disperse the centralized, metropolitan court system that had given him a field of action. The more secure city lawyers, on the other hand, did not struggle against the conciliation court; they merely saw little need for it when the best men in the profession were already doing their best to discourage litigation.[7]

Besides discussing codification and conciliation courts, the convention took up a proposal that all men of "good moral character" be entitled to admission to practice in all courts of the state. The man who pushed this was a farmer who had practiced as a part-time lawyer in the justices' courts, whose competence he also wished to extend. When he saw that a large part of the delegates (a third of the whole were lawyers) opposed so extreme a leveling of admission standards, he accepted one proposal to amend the requisite qualifications by adding "learning and ability" to mere "good moral character." The lawyer who drafted this revision insisted that the whole new set of requisites would still liberalize admission requirements, since it would prevent the courts from requiring any set period of legal education as a preliminary to examination.[8] This is, in fact, what happened when the provision went into effect along with the new constitution. But something else happened, too. The old study requirements had been connected, in a rough way, with the formal division of the New York bar into two grades: attorneys, who could practice only in certain lower courts, and counselors, who could practice in higher courts. This division had been one of the most obvious formal products of the efforts in the late eighteenth century to sharpen professional status. It now disappeared completely, even thongh no one had mentioned it in the convention debates.[9]

The debates that led to the new provision did churn up much rhetoric against lawyers. But the final vote that put it into the draft constitution did not divide men on simple occupational lines. The solid core of aye votes came from the same men who voted to impose nativist qualifications for the governorship. The antinativist group, however, disagreed among themselves on the matter of lawyers, with a significant number of New York city men, lawyers, and Irish voting for the provision.[10] Apparently its wording appealed to antilawyer feelings of the more home-conscious Yankee and Yorker farmers, while not offending either the sterner Yankee elements or the more complacent modern city men. The vote separated nativists from antinativists rather more clearly than it separated lawyers from farmers, since many lawyers accepted easily the demise of sharp professional status, and none defended the quasi-Federalist hierarchy implicit in the old system.

Contrasts between social fatalism and a sense of private worth appeared also in other professions. Take an incident already described, the discourse delivered by Edwards A. Park of Andover Seminary, to the Pastoral Association of Congregational Ministers in Massachusetts, on "peculiar duties which are incumbent on the New England clergy."[11] For the most part, he was urging "Puritan" ministers to resist popish practices as they appeared in the blandishments of the Episcopal high church. He did get some special public attention when a pamphleteer who claimed to be a Boston Anglo-Catholic issued a reply to some of Park's nativist remarks.[12] But in the course of his sermon Park made certain other points that he may not have intended for general consumption at all. He warned the ministers "to be circumspect in their treatment of the laity." He recognized that Congregational practice had always shown "a peculiar deference for laymen . . . But they must not thence be flattered into an overweening estimate of their capabilities . . . There are disputes pertaining to the nature of the will, to the relations of sin, which try the sagacity of the most sharp-sighted philosophers, and on which we should not invite the mechanic and the ploughman to pass a dogmatical decision. We should conduct our scholastic disputes in a scholastic way, and we do wrong to our own minds, when we carry our scientific difficulties down to the arena of popular dissension."[13] Having thus urged the ministers to forget about the traditional intellectual competence of New England congregations, he warned that serious theological sermons would only encourage the people to hunt heresy in their ministers. Rather than use learning in their pastoral work, ministers should cherish learning as a mark of status.[14]

Park was, quite consciously, arguing in two directions at once. His was the kind of whiggery that sought exclusiveness in a private intellectual sphere while seeking a solidarity with the nonintellectuals on carefully simplified issues. He was suggesting that the professional men to whom he spoke give up their old efforts to make all their professional activities into a high intellectual life. He urged that they accept their new function as nurses to the popular mind, salving their professional consciences with the knowledge of what high matters they pursued in private.

The meeting to which Park spoke produced one concrete move toward a new definition of ministerial status. Traditionally, a man could not be a Congregational minister unless he had been ordained as pastor of a particular local church; and in the strictest theory, if he ceased to be a local pastor, he ceased to be a minister.[15] A committee set up by this meeting allowed that men might be ordained "at large" if they were going into mission work, seminary teaching, or even college teaching. This recommendation came to nothing at that time. For all practical purposes, many Congregationalists were already indulging in just such bureaucratic ordination, but accepting an outright statement of the practice was another matter. Not until 1865 did representative Congregationalist bodies adopt the new idea.[16] The "action" they reached in the 1840's consisted in their simply being the kind of group within which Park's statement was conceivable. Some traits they shared with the New York City lawyers. They were receptive to the idea that there existed a peculiar link between accommodating themselves to popular ideas and pursuing their highest professional concerns in spheres removed from the public. But there was a difference. When a bar leader argued that New York lawyers should accept the simplified code of procedure that followed hard on the 1846 convention, he insisted that the loss of arcane technicalities would only force lawyers to show the greater ability in applying true legal principles—that it would push them, in other words, along that path of legal rationalism that became clear in following decades of American law. But, however much Congregationalism may have fallen in with the growing tendency of denominations toward sameness and some rationalism, that was not quite the calling that Park heard for his audience. Rather, he wanted them to develop among themselves the complex positive substance of their profession.

This problem of the relation between the nature of professional science and the way a profession develops ap-

peared also in another incident, that involving Horace
Green and the medical profession of New York City. In
1847, the New York Medical and Surgical Society, one of
those small fraternities devoted to study and mutual help,
requested Green to resign from membership. Green, an
ambitious doctor from Vermont, had found in specialization the answer to his own career problem: how to build
a respectable city practice after having been trained to a
crude therapeutic standard in his home state. He had
worked out techniques for treating nose and throat dis-
eases, he had got a reputation for these techniques with
the lay public, and he had gradually given up general practice.[17] On top of this, he had seemed to seek attention by
making novel claims, especially by publicizing his instruments for introducing medication directly into the larynx.
Several established practitioners, including the surgeon
Valentine Mott, insisted that Green lied. When Green
presented testimony from his patients, the critics denounced him for injecting the laity into a professional
quarrel. And when he tried to demonstrate his procedure
in front of doctors, he did so with patients whom he had
not reassured adequately, and who therefore gagged on
the instrument. Then came the forced resignation.[18]

This incident, within one of the more exclusive medical
clubs of the city, provided a concrete illustration for
ideas that were at the same time involved in the reorgani-
zation of the whole medical community. Partly to replace
the official but moribund New York County Medical Society, regular New York physicians had just organized the
New York Academy of Medicine, a private organization in
its definition of membership, yet aiming to include something like all respectable practitioners. It was at this point
that John W. Francis called on Academy members to rise
above the factional disputes that had split New York

medicine for two generations. They should, among other things, forbear pressing "vainglorious" claims to "special merit" for their ideas.[19] This ideal and Green's case merged a few years later when Green's enemies came within a very few votes of expelling him from the Academy.[20]

These developments in the various professions in New York and Massachusetts fitted well with what professional men were saying about themselves around the middle of the century. Regularly the elegiac tone appeared: Our vocation is not what it was a generation ago, or fifty years ago. Then, no man ventured to take up our high duties unless he was known intimately to the great men already working in the field. Then, the texts that contained the knowledge of the field may not have been many, but no man ventured in unless he had mastered those texts. Once in, no man had the freedom to go wherever his whim took him, but he began work as a member of a structured corporate body that provided him with continuing sustenance and supervision. If he belonged to a Congregationalist or quasi-Congregationalist religious group, the corporate body was the individual church, in which the minister was expected to sink roots but which had its own roots in turn in the local community. If he belonged to a hierarchic group of the Methodist variety, he found in the circuit a directing context for his life. If, on the other hand, he was a lawyer, he practiced not as an individual selling his services to persons in a locality, but as a member of a bar that had its own identity. In many areas outside cities, judge and lawyers traveled together over the judicial circuit, operating as a club who knew each other far better than they knew the typical client.

Then, so the lament went, change had entered. The quality of persons who entered the profession declined. The time or seriousness that individuals put into preparation for their work fell off. And the peculiar social institutions by which each group maintained its morale, its discipline, and its quality fell into decay. Such large numbers of men entered each profession that a careless market relationship seemed the only means of regulating professional activity, since the older intimate groups were no longer commensurate to the new vocational populations. The last formal distinctions between different kinds or ranks of persons in one profession vanished. The separate rank of counselor disappeared from the bar in those states where it had survived. Physicians exerted strong pressure against the man who sought repute for himself as an individual rather than as a member of the profession. Among Protestants, the sectarian distinctions that had made one kind of minister different from another subsided into formalities as all approached the denominational norm. Even among evangelicals, the demand for a pious ministry merged into the manufacture of ministers by seminaries. Whether in the secular professions or even in hierarchic kinds of ministry, the professional leader became less the individual with legal or hierarchic or charismatic authority, more the individual who served as secretary or librarian or professor or editor in some service agency. Despite pious resolutions, an agency like the National Council of Congregational Churches, the American Medical Association, or the many professional schools then emerging found it easier to attend to its own identity than to promote or encourage or even sanction individual distinction among men who entered the profession. Each profession retained much of its sense of being a special in-group, yet seemed to move toward uniformity, away from any individual distinction other than what emerged from impersonal competition in the labor market that the profession itself became.

Much of whatever decline or ingrowing was real was involuntary. In the English-speaking world, hostility against the professions formed a part of antiaristocratic or dissenting or reformist rhetoric. Such rhetoric gained increasing acceptance in the United States over the first third of the nineteenth century. Upwardly mobile groups, including men who wanted access to professional standing on terms less stringent than had developed in the latter part of the eighteenth century, used this rhetoric as a weapon to open opportunities for themselves. In effect, they promised the public that it could split apart the traditional, tense bond between warm professional confidence and sharp professional authority. The public, it was said, could accept the Physician and reject the Doctor.[21] Legislatures in many states abolished compulsory medical licensure, withdrew recognition from medical associations, discarded hierarchic distinctions among lawyers, loosened restrictions on who could practice law, or weeded out mystifying common-law elements from the forms of legal practice. Congregations asserted preferences for a warmer, more exciting, but less authoritative ministry.

There is a difficulty, though, in ascribing all the decline in professional morale to attacks from below: often, conservative leaders rushed out to meet the levelers, or reinforced the leveling efforts in ways that did not appear to the public. Take the bar, for instance. In the years around 1800, when the sense of professional distinctiveness was near something of a peak, it was assumed even in a commercial center like New York that an unknown lawyer who had the ability to get ahead would begin to attract attention by eloquence in criminal trials. And even in the old Southwest, the fact that a man relied on the éclat of criminal practice did not prevent most of his actual work from being commercial practice. Nor did his acquiring practice through this tactic prevent his being accepted by local bar leaders, once he had acquired sufficient repute to make this surrender graceful.[22] Even though some writers feared lest "Irish" standards of bombastic eloquence be imported into American courts,[23] a Charles O'Conor made his way up through means little different from those used by many old American lawyers. By the 1850's, though, the patrician George Templeton Strong was writing that the New York bar included only three gentlemen, even if many more than that had built sizable practices. And by the 1860's and 1870's he complained that lawyers like O'Conor took a malign, antisocial delight in defending vicious criminals.[24] Nativism gave men a renewed language with which to define a barrier that had earlier existed most clearly in the means by which men surmounted it. Upward mobility became less proper even while it may have become more common. The process by which men like Strong put a negative value on the spectacular criminal lawyer implied a distaste for all the techniques of spectacular individual assertion in the profession.

This same defining had long worked among medical men. Back in the 1760's, when Samuel Bard had submerged the too obvious elements of his personal ambition in civic promotion, the individualistic role was taken up by Sir James Jay, who tried to establish himself as leader of the New York medical community against the opposition of the conservative, collective leadership. Jay failed; then, about 1790, the role of opposition leader was revived by Nicholas Romayne, who fought the Bard group off and on for twenty years. Part of the time he relied on political support from the lesser or marginal practitioners of the city, even though he had little real sympathy with their interests. Romayne failed, like Jay, but less because of strong conservative resistance than because a protégé of Bard's—

David Hosack—managed to play the two kinds of leadership against each other long enough to propel himself into what had been Jay's or Romayne's position in local medicine. Hosack dominated the medical community for twenty years, to the increasing frustration of Bard's pupils and friends, who accepted the old pattern of collective leadership and denounced Hosack as an ingrate and a veritable personality cultist.[25] They published bitter complaints against the ways some physicians attracted attention to themselves, attacking not only outright vulgarity and commercialism but also the use of the general press and the lecture platform as media for approaching the public.[26] The complainants—that is, the legitimate professional descendants of Bard—had influence in the New York State Medical Society in 1823, when that society adopted a code of ethics that first laid a clear ban on physicians' advertising as well as on the airing of medical controversies in the lay press.[27] Bard's "descendants" also acted to organize small medical fraternities that would provide them with havens away from the larger medical community. It was, ultimately, one of these clubs that expelled Horace Green in 1847.[28] The conflict between sober collective leadership and flamboyant individual assertion had a continuous history in the local medical community. During the years when there was much new assertion of professional status to absorb the energies of all leaders, the conflict usually got resolved short of explosion. But when Hosack won out and the balance of influence turned against the conservative leaders, they in turn mobilized against him an envy that showed all the signs of upper-class anti-intellectualism.

Among clergymen, two different kinds of conservative pressure operated close to the center of professional power: pressure from the established leaders, be they bishops in

the hierarchic churches or men like Ezra Stiles and Lyman
Beecher and Horace Bushnell on the Congregational side;
and pressure from propertied laymen. In resisting the influence of evangelists, the established clerics acted much as
did leaders in other professions who set their backs against
a lecturing physician or a picaresque criminal lawyer.
But whether prominent laymen also supported the resistance to evangelical assertion depended on the structure of the particular community and on the structure of
the particular religious group. Among New York Methodists, propertied men seem to have backed the fragmentation of circuits into individual churches and thus to have
challenged the central authority of both circuits and bishops. Among New York State Episcopalians, it was wealthy
local churches that most resisted the centralizing efforts of
Bishop Hobart. But, although a few Episcopalians of standing backed moves to transfer some ritual functions to laymen, the more substantial Methodists resisted any move
to open up slots in the church schedule for lay preachers.[29]
In general, conservative laymen resisted both individual
assertion by evangelists and individual leadership by clerics
who laid claim to hierarchic or permanent status within
the community. Since a part of conservative clerical influence also operated against individual assertion, the
bulk of conservative leadership within the churches worked
to limit individual achievement as a professional value.
Even the convergence of various churches on the denominational pattern in these years, which was incidentally
a means of professional defense against the laity, encouraged standardization of performance among clerics.

In these situations, "leadership" or "achievement" cuts
two different ways, even while seeming always the opposite
of mediocrity. If men in the learned professions, if even
men near the top of the learned professions, had been

united on what they believed professional leadership should be and on what men could legitimately do to demonstrate professional eminence, then democratic influence might not have prevailed against the professions in the second quarter of the nineteenth century. Men were willing to slap down the efforts of some extraordinary individuals because those efforts endangered group leadership. If mediocrity includes a strengthening of the merely respectable at the expense of the salient individual, then professional leaders bore quite as real a responsibility as did any Jacksonian populace for what happened to their groups.

One thing may excuse this aspect of mediocrity. The content of professional knowledge was neither stable nor securely progressive. In medicine, for instance, men knew that they were leaving behind the academic theories, the comprehensive theories, the individualistic theories of earlier years. They had a much less clear idea about where their science was going, and about how a medical individualist might reasonably behave. If they had consciously planned to declare a moratorium on idiosyncrasy, in order to gain time for new standards to become rooted, they could hardly have found means more apt than those physicians did in fact use. Clergymen, too, needed some respite within which to recover from the intellectual disorder of the immediate past. Lawyers admitted that they hoped to find new standards of professional behavior within the very reforms that simplified or eliminated traditional modes of practice. All somehow shunted individual achievement aside, concealing it from public inspection. One test for the justifiability of this tactic lay in two questions: did each group in fact progress toward objectivity, and did that objectivity become a secure base, taken for granted, on which a new and productive individualism could build?

The various professions could not meet this test in the same manner, even if they should all meet it satisfactorily. They had not, after all, manifested their reactions against public individualism in the same way. The heart of the difference on this point lay in the differences between their fields of knowledge. For Americans, at least, the law was becoming a field that men themselves created according to their positive wishes. This is one reason why lawyers who accepted the leveling moves of the period turned much more toward private individualism, and less toward private group activity, than did physicians or clergymen.[30] The ultimate standard for what was true in legal knowledge lay in what the state or the public wanted, not in a scientific or transcendent perception to which men had to train their faculties. Physicians and clergymen, precisely because they dealt with truths that did not depend on conscious human choice, had rather more need to handle their intellectual problems through groups that afforded support and authority. There is a sociology of knowledge, certainly. There is also an epistemology of social groups: what a profession was trying to know had some effect on how it could react to outside events.

To the extent that the professions did meet successfully the need for a renewed and productive objectivity, the climate of mediocrity—in the sense of a dampening of both intellectual arrogance and intellectual individualism—was a stage through which they passed on the way to a bureaucratic resolution of earlier problems. In a more communal America, the very fact that professional men had lived with close access to the substance of social power had given a dangerous or threatening quality to their ideas on even abstruse professional matters. Professionals seemed then to have the ability to make their least ideas matter. Popular and even intraprofessional apprehensions about such power helped to block a full, dispassionate dealing with ideas that might lead to professional usefulness. In time, though, the depersonalizing of ideas, disconnecting them as far as possible from individual prestige or social allegiance, promoted the emergence of professional structures that seemed to exist alongside the central social structure, serving it but not partaking of it. Within such structures, the stimuli to intellectual achievement could regain force without seeming to offer a new threat.

Inertia helped to sustain quality during the transitional phase. Just as the rationalistic multivolume intellectuals of late Victorian England seemed to operate on fires of moral energy that had been banked by an earlier, evangelical generation, so the best American professionals of the mid-nineteenth century worked on an inculcated obligation to quality. They worked toward goals in knowledge and practice for which their immediate environment provided relatively little incentive, either by enforcing standards or by lavishing attention upon the achievers. Such momentum accounts for much of the intellectual product of Boston Unitarians during the years after the Unitarian coup had become an old story. It also accounts for some Boston arrogance about the morale of its medical profession. Medical spokesmen in other areas complained that, whenever more than a very few physicians practiced in one community, they fell into vicious methods of competing with each other. When a Boston medical editor said that Boston had no such problem, and was asked how this could be, he answered only, in essence, "We behave like gentlemen."[31] There was almost certainly less self-restraint in the Boston community than its spokesman claimed, and what he praised was probably all too often a corpse-cold gentility like unto corpse-cold Unitarianism. But the moral momentum of the period was real enough, and was hardly confined to those communities that specialized in it.

The difficulty is that inertia, even in movement, lacks true self-propulsion or intensity. The dampening of individual reward, followed hard by a salutary bureaucracy, could only strike men as a victory for half of the old inspiration-or-nurture issue that the earliest American feeling had kept suspended in a bond that was half theology, half metaphysical conceit. Attempts to recoup the loss of intensity began early. They showed in the ability of summer-colony intellectuals like Hawthorne or Bryant to romanticize a decaying rural back country into a refuge of the true America.[32] They showed in the way that Josephus C. Guild made his whole legal career in Tennessee a sentimentalized gesture toward retrospect. They showed in the historicism and local antiquarianism that some ministers began to display from the middle years of the nineteenth century on, and in the success with which such historicism assured them security in local niches. They showed, too, in the way that rationalizations for the outdoor life helped feed the refurbishing of the professional military role, toward the end of the century.

The attempts at reviving the intensity of professional life, which were of course part of a broader response directed at the tone or style of all American life, proceeded on two levels. Especially at first, the efforts were crude and sentimental; this level has continued into the twentieth century in recurrent versions of the Strenuous Life, in popular doting on military arrogance, and in forlorn efforts by foundations to encourage nonconformism or to revive the prestige of criminal lawyers. But in recent years a more serious level has taken form, in the neo-orthodoxy of some Protestant theology, in the kind of new conservatism that has discovered subtlety in legal thinkers of the Adams-Marshall-Kent generation, and in the efforts that professional schools have made to instill some sense of values or community responsibility into young lawyers or doctors or business administrators.

In the context of these two levels of effort to renew intensity, there is a close resemblance between the controversies over civil-military relations in the twentieth century and the quarrels over disciplining antinomians or revivalists or medical experimenters in earlier years. In its arguments, the military right has drawn some implicit benefit from the older polemics in favor of a converted ministry. It has been able to suggest, truthfully enough, that efforts to restrict the military have been part of a long tendency for ordinary leaders to restrict the honest or the inspired individual. But that this repression of individualism has been equally evil in all contexts is the arguable assumption. Enthusiasm, as a form of antiprofessional behavior within a profession, has often had a valuable social function. This does not mean that it always has that function. One may accept, for purposes of argument, the thesis that Andrew Jackson acted rightly in entering Spanish Florida and, on his own authority in peacetime, there executing two British subjects whom he judged to have conspired with Indians against Americans. One may sympathize with the blooded legalism of a Josephus Guild attacking an enemy in the flesh and accepting the consequences. But one may also note that the experimental boldness of a Horace Green carried with it a willingness to make jokes about how he built his early practice on therapeutic methods that impressed while nearly killing his patients— a willingness like the ease with which Americans of good will can find fun in the neatness of vigilante justice.

The underlying issue between vigor and discipline has never, in American life, stayed settled for long. The continued life of the issue is in fact one of the virtues of the bureaucratic or technological resolution that seemed to dispose of many problems within the professions around the middle of the nineteenth century. The turn toward bureaucratic impersonality arose from a need for social arrangements that would bypass earlier quarrels. It achieved some degree of order without imposing outright coercion and without moving the professions as close to the substance of social authority as they had tended during parts of the eighteenth century. One of the questions about the twentieth-century development of the professions will be: are these technically neutral structures that were formed a century ago going to ossify, becoming meaningful only as any serviceable special-interest group is meaningful; or, are they being resorbed into the main areas of social power? Both views have been argued by the apostles of sociological apprehension. That such men have exaggerated, and that skepticism is suggested by comparison with such other controversies as that over the changing degree of business concentration in American society, do not lessen the importance of the issues. In an earlier period, individuals and groups took varying, inconsistent positions on the conflict between the need for quality and the danger of aristocracy. Of course, neither aristocracy nor uniformly high achievement was ever very likely. Achievement and aristocracy were instead general standards by which one could judge how particular groups fitted into changes of social style. Even now, the statements of apprehension are often ridiculous. But the terms of apprehension—neutrality, power, sterility, privilege—are points at which history feeds into judgment on the course of professional life.

Notes

Chapter I. Power, Responsibility, and Style

1. See the versions of Patrick Darby's law career presented in Jo. C. Guild, *Old Times in Tennessee* (Nashville, 1878), pp. 460-461; and in Thomas Perkins Abernethy, *From Frontier to Plantation in Tennessee* (Chapel Hill, 1932), pp. 265-268.

2. Horace Green told stories on himself as a beginning practitioner in Vermont. In one case he prescribed an overdose of sulphuric ether for cholera morbus. The patient recovered anyway, the family praised Green for seeing the need "to administer a most powerful remedy," and the town gave him a quick reputation for "a most wonderful cure." MS Autobiography, pp. 54-59, New York Academy of Medicine Library.

3. This estimate is low, if judged by the fact that the nineteenth-century ratio of physicians to population approached twice that for more recent generations. It takes account of the thinner population and more isolated dwellings of earlier generations. Good occupational censuses, broken down by the actual communities in which people lived, are rare; but see *Census of the State of New-York, for 1845* (Albany, 1846); and Massachusetts Bureau of Statistics of Labor, *The Census of Massachusetts, 1885, I: Population and Social Statistics,* pt. 2 (Boston, 1888), pp. xxxvi, 4-34, 36, 416.

4. The following ranking, contained in a review article on Chancellor Kent, is even more exceptional than its inclusion of the military at all: "Divinity, medicine, arms, are perhaps the most important of what are usually called the professions; but those who know that the profession of law has always furnished the most zealous assertors and defenders of liberty in this and other countries, cannot believe it far behind the others in utility." *Atlantic Magazine* (New York), I (1824), 148-149.

Chapter II. Fear of Individuality: John W. Francis and the New York Medical Community

1. John W. Francis, *Anniversary Discourse before the New-York Academy of Medicine. Delivered in the Broadway Taber-*

nacle, November 10, 1847 (New York, 1847); John W. Francis, *An Inaugural Address. Delivered before the New-York Academy of Medicine, February 2, 1848* (New York, 1848).

2. On the background of the New York Academy of Medicine, see Richard H. Shryock, *American Medical Research, Past and Present* (New York, 1947), pp. 28-34; and Philip Van Ingen, *The New York Academy of Medicine* (New York, 1949), 15. On societies outside New York, see *New York Journal of Medicine*, X (1848), 108-110, 247-251.

3. Henry T. Tuckerman, "John W. Francis," in John W. Francis, *Old New York* (New York, 1865), pp. xxiv, xxvii, xxx-xxxii, ci. Tuckerman saw his subject in a light that Francis' statements of 1847-48 almost negate: "Probably no American physician was ever regarded from more extreme points of partiality and prejudice than Dr. Francis; the fact, to those familiar with the philosophy of local reputation and of character, is the best evidence of original merit: only those who have the intellect to conceive and the courage to follow vigorous and intelligent principles, are subject to such diversity of opinion; the devotee of precedent, the theoretical bigot, and the compromising and conciliating votary of any and all the liberal professions, enjoys a certain mediocre respectability, and therefore excites neither warm commendation nor severe criticism; he is like the negative characters whom Dante's guide refused to discuss, and disposed of with a passing look" (p. xxiii). But on the prudential strain in Francis' attitude, see his papers in the New York Public Library, especially the draft of a letter to David Hosack, May 26, 1816.

4. J. W. Francis to [Hosack?], draft, Albany, April 10, 1815, New York Public Library; T. Romeyn to Francis, ca. October 1813, Oct. 29, 1813, Feb. 16, 1815, and March (n.d.), New York State Library.

5. Sholto Douglas, *Some Account of a Secret Society in New-York, entitled the "Kappa-Lambda"* (New York, 1859), pp. 12-13.

6. Susan Hayes Ward, *The History of the Broadway Tabernacle* (New York, 1901), pp. 69, 78-80; Augustus K. Gardner, *Eulogy of John W. Francis* (New York, 1861), pp. 12-13.

7. Francis, *Anniversary Discourse*, pp. 38-39.

8. *Ibid.*, pp. 16, 20-21.

9. *Ibid.*, p. 74.

10. Francis, *Inaugural Address*, p. 13.

11. *Ibid.*, pp. 7, 9, 10, 14.

12. *Ibid.*, pp. 9-10. Compare the perceptive discussion of twentieth-century developments in the problem of "anonymity" and the

reporting of medical news, in Robert D. Potter, "New Horizons and New Problems," *New York Medicine*, XII (1956), 308-310.

13. Other speakers to the Academy followed the same general line, even if not with Francis' intensity. See especially John Stearns, *An Address, Delivered on the Occasion of Assuming the Chair as President* (New York, 1847), pp. 8, 11-13.

14. See, for example, John Bard, "An Essay on the Nature and Cause of that Malignant Pleurisy," which proved so remarkably fatal to the Inhabitants of Huntington, and some other places on Long-Island; in the Winter of the Year 1749. Drawn up at the request of a Weekly Society of Gentlemen in New York, and Addressed to them at one of their Meetings. New York, January, 1749," MS, New York Academy of Medicine Library. Peter Middleton, *A Medical Discourse, or an Historical Inquiry into the Ancient and Present State of Medicine* (New York, 1769), pp. 67-69.

15. S[amuel] B[ard] to [John Bard], September 4, [1763], Bard Papers, New York Academy of Medicine; John Bard to Samuel Bard, January [17], 1764, Bard Papers, Bard College; Sir James Jay to James Duane, March 12, 1764, New-York Historical Society; Brooke Hindle, *The Pursuit of Science in Revolutionary America, 1735-1789* (Chapel Hill, 1956), pp. 117-119.

16. Excerpts from record book of the Medical Society of 1782-83, typescript, New-York Historical Society.

17. "Minutes of the Medical Society of the State of New York, from its organization, November 14, 1794 to January 13, 1806," New York Academy of Medicine Library; important excerpts from this book of minutes are published in James J. Walsh, *History of the Medical Society of the State of New York* (n.p., 1907), pp. 36-54. See also Samuel L. Mitchill, *A Discourse on the Life and Character of Samuel Bard* (New York, 1821), p. 18.

18. Jules Calvin Ladenheim, " 'The Doctors' Mob' of 1788," *Journal of the History of Medicine and Allied Sciences,* V (1950), 23-43.

19. So Thomas Cock remembered the situation many years later: *Inaugural Address, Delivered before the New York Academy of Medicine* (New York, 1852), p. 9. See also the address by James R. Manley in Medical Society of the State of New York, *Transactions . . . from Its Organization in 1807, up to and Including 1831* (Albany, 1868), pp. 390-391n.

20. On the upstate origins of the 1806 laws, see Stearns's paper in Medical Society of the County of New York, Minutes, Sept. 10, 1827. The text and later publication history of this paper are presented in Walsh, *History of the Medical Society of the State of*

New York, pp. 56-61. The Minutes and other early records of the County Society are on deposit at the New York Academy of Medicine. Their completeness and continuity show the effort that New York physicians made to preserve a group life in the early decades of the century, despite disruptive crosscurrents in medical life.

21. Medical Society of the County of New York, Minutes, July 2, 1806.

22. *Ibid.,* Jan. 5, Feb. 19, March 23, 1807, April 25, Oct. 3, 1808, Jan. 7, 1809, Dec. 21, 1819; Nicholas Romayne, *Report and Address, Delivered by the President, to the Medical Society of the County of New-York* (New York, 1807).

23. See David Hosack, *Observations on the Establishment of the College of Physicians and Surgeons in the City of New-York* (New York, 1811).

24. See, for instance, Hosack's advice that his students not imitate the versatility of Benjamin Rush, in "Observations on the Medical Character . . . 1826," *Essays on Various Subjects of Medical Science,* III (New York, 1830), 119-120. The change in his conscious attitude may have been extremely gradual, since Rush's example is recommended to reluctant students as late as Hosack and Francis' *American Medical and Philosophical Register,* IV (1813-14), 15. And in 1820 a writer hostile to Hosack's influence argued: "The observation of every one will recognize the truth of the remark, that physicians who manifest a remarkable partiality for any of the departments of natural history, or who pursue any collateral branch of knowledge with ardor, have never possessed any very exalted view of their profession, or been distinguished for the profoundness of their science, or the nicety of their practical skill" *(New York Literary Journal,* vol. III, 1820, p. 83).

25. Medical Society of the County of New York, Minutes, Jan. 4, 18, Feb. 20, March 6, Dec. 21, 28, 1819, May 8, 1820; Hosack to Francis, [June 2, 4, 1819], New York State Library.

26. Chauncey D. Leake, "What Was Kappa Lambda?" *Annals of Medical History,* 1st ser., IV (1922), 198; Lee D. Van Antwerp, "Kappa Lambda, Elf or Ogre?" *Bulletin of the History of Medicine,* XVII (1945), 327-350; Philip Van Ingen, "Remarks on 'Kappa Lambda, Elf or Ogre' and a Little More Concerning the Society," *ibid.,* pp. 513-538.

27. For John W. Francis' opposition to this requirement of the law, see *American Medical and Philosophical Register,* III (1812-13), 86-87.

28. Medical Society of the County of New York, Minutes, July 7, 1806, and "Bye-Laws," Minutes, I, 19-23.

29. *Ibid.,* Minutes, July 2, 1810.

30. *Ibid.,* July 6, 1819.

31. Samuel Smith Purple, "Biographical Sketch of the Life of Dr. John Stearns," p. 15, MS, New York Academy of Medicine Library.

32. For a suggestive analysis of the difference between rural and urban fee structures, see George Rosen, *Fees and Fee Bills,* Supplement to the *Bulletin of the History of Medicine,* No. 6 (Baltimore, 1946), p. 11.

33. *A System of Medical Ethics, Published by Order of the Medical Society of New York* (New York, 1823), p. 13, and see pp. 3-4, 9-10, 17.

34. Medical Society of the County of New York, Comitia Minora Minutes, Aug. 6, 1828, Sept. 16, 1833, Nov. 4, 1840, and Society Minutes, Dec. 9, 1833, citing Attorney-General Greene C. Bronson's opinion in Medical Society of the State of New York, *Transactions,* I (1832-33), appendix, pp. 76-77.

35. Medical Society of the County of New York, Minutes, June 13, July 7, Aug. 8, 22, Sept. 12, Oct. 10, 1825, and Comitia Minora Minutes, Jan. 5, 26, May 4, June 8, Aug. 3, Oct. 5, 1825.

36. *Ibid.,* Comitia Minora Minutes, Dec. 5, 1832, and Society Minutes, Dec. 17, 1832.

37. "Roll of Medical Society of the County of New York Jany 1st 1830," Medical Society of the County of New York, Minutes, I, 438.

38. On the serious intellectual pretensions of the first homeopaths see John F. Gray, *The Early Annals of Homeopathy in New York* (New York, 1863), pp. 13, 18-19, 22-23; and *Homeopathy in New-York, and the Late Abraham D. Wilson* (New York, 1865), pp. 10-11.

39. On the relation of medical politics to general politics in New York, see Walter Hugins, *Jacksonian Democracy and the Working Class: A Study of the New York Workingmen's Movement, 1829-1837* (Stanford, 1960), pp. 1-2, 106, 166-170.

40. Medical Society of the County of New York, Minutes, Aug. 8, Sept. 19, 23, 1831, Feb. 13, 1832.

41. *Ibid.,* Nov. 7, 1831; "Medical Society Report of the Committee Appointed to Draft a Circular, New-York School of Medicine," undated handbill in New York Academy of Medicine Library.

42. Medical Society of the County of New York: Comitia Minora Minutes, Sept. 16, Nov. 6, Dec. 7, 21, 1833, and Society Minutes, Oct. 6, 1831, March 12, April 9, May 25, Sept. 21, 1832, Jan. 18, July 8, 15, Sept. 16, Dec. 9, 16, 23, 30, 1833.

43. Frederick C. Waite, "The First Medical Diploma Mill in the United States," *Bulletin of the History of Medicine,* XX (1946), 503.

44. Medical Society of the County of New York: Comitia

Minora Minutes, March 19, 21, 1836, and Society Minutes, Oct. 8, 15, 1835, Feb. 18, 1836. See also Gray, *Early Annals of Homeopathy in New York,* 16-17; *United States Medical and Surgical Journal,* I (1834-35), 465. But note that homeopathic influence did not prevent the Society from rejecting further candidates who presented Christian College diplomas (Comitia Minora Minutes, May 4, June 16, 1836).

45. This pattern actually began as early as June 9, 1834, but was interrupted by the year of homeopathic influence. On July 27, 1840, the Society abandoned a quorum for nonbusiness meetings, and on August 10 it reduced the quorum for business meetings from 25 to 21.

46. *New York Journal of Medicine,* VII (1846), 409-410; *New York Medical and Surgical Reporter,* I (1845-46), 392-394, 405-408.

47. The dynamics of this sequence of events was described explicitly by Thomas Cock in 1852, although Cock's memory telescoped many of the events after 1806 (*Inaugural Address,* p. 15).

48. For an argument that the real danger of quackery came from "degenerate" members within the regular profession, see F. Campbell Stewart, "The Actual Condition of the Medical Profession in This Country," *New York Journal of Medicine,* VI (1846), 169-170.

49. *American Monthly Magazine and Critical Review,* IV (1818-19), 479-480.

50. George H. Tucker, *Medical Register of the City of New-York* (New York, 1862); *New York Journal of Medicine and Surgery,* II (1840), 248; *Constitution and By-Laws of the Physico-Medical Society of New-York* (New York, 1817), pp. 3-5, 10.

51. Philip Van Ingen, *A Brief Account of the First One Hundred Years of the New York Medical and Surgical Society* (Richmond, Va., 1946), pp. 8-10, 17-18; *New York Journal of Medicine and Surgery,* I (1839), 204-209.

52. Columbia Medical Society, Minutes, New York State Library; M. S. Lloyd, "The First One Hundred Years of the Richmond County Medical Society," *New York Journal of Medicine,* LIV (1954), 698-702, esp. p. 700 for citation of a bylaw penalizing consultation with any physician outside the society unless the patient had refused every member of the local society.

53. Minutes of the Medical Society, pp. 18-19, 43; *An Account of the New-York Hospital* (New York, 1811), p. 6.

54. Columbia County Medical Society, Minutes, New York State Library; Medical Society of the County of New York, Minutes, Dec. 28, 1819, Sept. 13, 1824, Dec. 12, 1825, Jan. 22, 1827, Dec. 12, 1831, Sept. 9, 1833; Hosack, *Essays,* III, 53-54.

55. Philip Van Ingen, "The Library without a Home," *Academy Bookman*, I, No. 2 (1948), 2-7.

56. *Report of the Committee Appointed by the Medical Society, of the State of New York, to Enquire into . . . the Pestilential Disease, That Prevailed in New-York during the Summer and Autumn of the year 1798* (New York, 1799).

57. Medical Society of the County of New York, Comitia Minora Minutes, June 21, 1820, and Society Minutes, May 8, Oct. 2, Nov. 27, 1820, June 15, 26, 29, 1832; Mitchill, *Discourse on the Life and Character of Samuel Bard*, pp. 30-32; A[lexander] C[oventry] to Editors of Edinburgh Medical and Surgical Journal, in *The Plough Boy* (Albany), II (1820-21), 313-315, 323-324; Richard H. Shryock, "The Yellow Fever Epidemics, 1793-1805," in Daniel Aaron, ed., *America in Crisis* (New York, 1952), pp. 51-70.

58. Medical Society of the County of New York, Minutes, Dec. 12, 1820; Hosack, "Observations on the Means of Improving the Medical Police of the City of New-York . . . 1820," *Essays*, II (New York, 1824), 9-86.

59. [Stearns], "Ms on the Epidemic Cholera of 1832," New York Academy of Medicine Library, MS. 170. Stearns did not merely imagine that conservatives blamed the panic on "young physicians" trying to "make practice"; compare *Letters from John Pintard*, New-York Historical Society Collections (New York, 1940-41), IV, 70; and Charles E. Rosenberg, "The Cholera Epidemic of 1832 in New York City," *Bulletin of the History of Medicine*, XXX (1959), 37-49.

60. *Report of the Committee of the Kappa Lambda Society, Appointed for the Purpose of Preparing an Account of the Mode of Treatment of Epidemic Cholera* (New York, 1832); Gray, *Homeopathy in New-York, and the Late Abraham D. Wilson*, p. 23.

61. Peter Middleton, *A Medical Discourse, or an Historical Inquiry into the Ancient and Present State of Medicine* (New York, 1769), pp. 67-69.

62. Quoted in Chauncey D. Leake, "A Gentleman Physician of New York: Dr. David Hosack, the Great American Practitioner of the Early Nineteenth Century," typescript, 1947, in New York Academy of Medicine Library.

63. Hosack, *Essays*, III, 126-130.

64. Colden to Dr. Samuel Mitchill, Nov. 7, [1745], *Letters and Papers of Cadwallader Colden*, New-York Historical Society Collections (New York, 1918-1937), VIII, 329.

65. Henry William Ducachet, *A Biographical Memoir of Samuel Bard* (Philadelphia, 1821), p. 23n.

66. *American Athenaeum*, I (1825), 380; F. Campbell Stewart,

"The Actual Condition of the Medical Profession in This Country," pp. 159-162. See also John Watson, "A Summary View of the Progress of Medicine in America," *New York Journal of Medicine and Surgery*, I (1839), 22; and *New-York Monthly Chronicle of Medicine and Surgery*, I (1824-25), 65-68.

67. James R. Manley, "Annual Address Delivered before the Medical Society of the State of New-York . . . February 8, 1826," *New-York Medical and Physical Journal*, V (1826), 9-10.

68. Van Ingen, *Brief Account of . . . the New York Medical and Surgical Society*, pp. 17, 22-23.

69. Caleb Ticknor, *A Popular Treatise on Medical Philosophy; or, an Exposition of Quackery and Imposture in Medicine* (New York, 1838), pp. 253-254, 257.

70. J. Watson, in *New York Journal of Medicine and Surgery*, I (1839), 191-192.

71. Horace Green, MS Autobiography, New York Academy of Medicine Library; L. R. March to Horace Green, July, 1855, MS. 662, New York Academy of Medicine Library; Van Ingen, *Brief History of . . . the New York Medical and Surgical Society*, pp. 38-44; "Dr. Horace Green and His Method," *Harper's Weekly*, Feb. 8, 1859; William Snow Miller, "Horace Green and His Probang," *Johns Hopkins Hospital Bulletin*, XXX (1919), 246-252.

72. Alex Berman, "Social Roots of the 19th Century Botanico-Medical Movement in the United States," *Actes du VIIIᵉ Congrès internationale d'histoire des sciences* (Florence, 1956), pp. 561-563.

73. Stewart, "The Actual Condition of the Medical Profession in This Country," p. 152; F.C.S., review of H. A. Boardman, *The Claims of Religion upon Medical Men* (Philadelphia, 1844), in *New York Journal of Medicine*, IV (1845), 86-90.

74. Ticknor, *Popular Treatise on Medical Philosophy*, pp. 257-258, 265; *New York Medical Gazette*, II (1842), 86-89, 184-185, 310; Horace Green, Autobiography; T. Romeyn Beck, *On the Utility of Country Medical Institutions* (Albany, 1825), pp. 8-9.

75. *United States Medical and Surgical Journal*, II (1835-36), 208.

Chapter III. Branding Iron and Retrospect: Lawyers in the Cumberland River Country

1. Sumner County Circuit Court, Minutes, 1838-1840, pp. 419, 427. The Summer County Court Minutes and other records are in the Sumner County Court House, Gallatin, Tennessee.

2. W. W. Clayton, *History of Davidson County, Tennessee* (Philadelphia, 1880), pp. 392-394.

3. J. C. Guild, *Old Times in Tennessee* (Nashville, 1878), p. 71.

4. *Ibid.*, pp. 67-91, 113-121.

5. Clayton, *Davidson County*, 108. Catron combined professional dignity with a plainer approach, as when his basic values showed through his opinion supporting disbarment of a lawyer for killing in a duel: the law, he said, aims to "restrain the blind and criminal passions that draw to ruin the fearless and valuable man; to restrain the wicked vanity of the noisy coxcomb; and to protect from his misguided fears of giddy and idle ridicule the physically weak and nervous man" (Joshua W. Caldwell, *Sketches of the Bench and Bar*, Knoxville, Tenn., 1898, p. 89).

6. William Nisbet Chambers, *Old Bullion Benton* (Boston, 1956), pp. 22-24; John Theodore Horton, *James Kent* (New York, 1939), pp. 123-139; and see especially James Willard Hurst, *The Growth of American Law: The Law Makers* (Boston, 1950), ch. 13, "The Uses of the Bar"; and William Francis English, *The Pioneer Lawyer and Jurist in Missouri*, University of Missouri Studies, vol. 21, no. 2 (Columbia, [Mo.], 1947). These last two studies contribute both detail and ideas that qualify the circuit-bar notion.

7. Caldwell, *Sketches*, pp. 71-73.

8. In the construction of tables based on these records, the following practical rules were observed. (1) The first court term in every year ending in zero was selected as a sample; but if the number of useful entries provided by this term was too small, then all the terms of that year were used. (2) Separate names were entered for every significant spelling variation and for every different partnership combination; only cautiously were initials expanded or variant forms equated.

9. Records of Davidson Co. County Court, Minute Book Vol. A, pp. 334-399, WPA transcript, Tennessee State Library.

10. Sumner Co. County Court, Minutes, I, 22-30.

11. Records of Davidson Co. County Court, Minute Book C, 220-240, microfilm in Tennessee State Library.

12. Sumner Co. County Court, Minutes, I, 238-281.

13. Records of Smith Co. Court of Pleas and Quarter Sessions, Minute Book, 1799-1800, pp. 1-59, Smith County Court House, Carthage, Tennessee, with WPA transcript in Tennessee State Library.

14. *Tennessee Gazette* (Nashville), Nov. [i.e., Dec.] 2, 1801.

15. "Minutes of the Superior Court of North Carolina Including Mero District, 1788-1803," pp. 265-336, WPA transcript, Tennessee State Library.

16. Davidson Co. Court, Minutes, Book G, 1809-1811, pp. 15-112, microfilm in Tennessee State Library. In the minutes a few *ad hoc*

partnerships appear; the members of these are counted separately in the table.

17. Sumner Co. County Court, Minutes, 1808-1812, pp. 181-211.

18. Thomas Hart Benton articles, reprinted in Robert H. White, ed., *Messages of the Governors of Tennessee, 1796-1821* (Nashville, 1952), pp. 299-300.

19. Emmerson to Overton, Feb. 19, 1809; Jan. 14, 1810; June 17, Aug. 19, 1811; June 30, Dec. 26, 1812; Sept. 18, 1813; Jan. 17, March 14, 1814; July 24, 1815; Jan. 27, Sept. 11, 1816; March 30, 1818; Overton Papers, Tennessee State Library.

20. S[amuel] Powel to Overton, Oct. 20, 1810 and April 29, 1811, *ibid.*

21. This argument assumes that the conveniences and needs of practice would affect the kind of pressures that lawyers would bring to bear on the structure of the judicial system. Rationalization being a devious process, such a point might not often appear in public argument; but note the related complaint made by William Carroll in explaining the court congestion of 1821: "Judges adjourn court from time to time to accommodate lawyers at Clarksville, Murfreesboro, etc." Quoted in Robert H. White, "Legislative Fathers of Our Judiciary," *Tennessee Law Review*, XXIII (1953-55), 11.

22. James Darrack to Robert Whyte, March 15, 1809, Whyte Papers, Tennessee State Library; Jackson and Hatchings to George Bartlett, Aug. 6, 1808, Andrew Jackson Papers, Library of Congress, microfilm in Tennessee State Library.

23. Emmerson to Overton, Jan. 14, 1810, Overton Papers, Tennessee State Library.

24. Davidson Co. Circuit Court, Appearance Docket, January Term 1840, Davidson Co. Court House, Nashville, Tennessee.

25. Sumner Co. Circuit Court, Minutes, 1839-1841, Record Book B, pp. 63-135, County Court Clerk's Office, Sumner Co. Court House.

26. Chancery Rule Docket, 1837-1841, Rules 152-193, Sumner Co. Court House.

27. Chancery Enrolling Docket, 1840-1841, Entries 1-246, *ibid.*

28. Eastin Morris, *Tennessee Gazetteer* (Nashville, 1834), pp. lxviii-lxviv, 26, 58-59, 149-50.

29. Smith Co. Circuit Court, Law Docket, 1836-1840, pp. 167-88, Smith Co. Court House.

30. Sumner Co. Chancery Court, Rule Docket, 1858-1862, pp. 268-494.

31. Davidson Co. Circuit Court, Appearance Docket, January Term 1860, Davidson Co. Court House.

32. These generalizations apply also to several dockets that are not summarized in tables here. In particular, the dockets available for 1850 form series consistent with the 1840 and 1860 dockets.

33. Tennessee Supreme Court, Trial Docket, 1836-1857, Tennessee State Library.

34. Tennessee Supreme Court, Trial Docket, 1858-1861 and 1873-1874, *ibid.*

35. See, for instance, the *National Gazette and Literary Register* (Philadelphia), Jan. 2, 1830.

36. These generalizations are based on samplings of Nashville, Gallatin, and Carthage newspapers from the following periods. Nashville: *Tennessee Gazette and Mero-District Advertiser*, 1800-1804; *Whig*, 1812-1820, 1840; *Republican and State Gazette*, 1830; *Union*, 1840; *Daily Republican Banner*, 1840, 1850, 1860. Gallatin: unknown paper, fragment from January 1820; *Journal*, 1827-1829; *Union and Sumner Advertiser*, 1832-1843; *Republican Sentinel*, 1840; *Tenth Legion*, 1849; *Courier*, 1861; *Examiner*, 1860-1890. Carthage: *Western Express*, 1808; *Gazette*, 1810-1824; *Tennessee Republican*, 1824-1825; *Farmer's Advocate*, 1832-1833; *Herald*, 1836; *Republican*, 1842-1845; *Mirror*, 1846. Except for the Nashville *Union and Whig*, all papers were used in the original or on microfilm at the Tennessee State Library; the *Union* and *Whig* were found at the Nashville Public Library.

37. Guild, *Old Times in Tennessee*, pp. 73, 460-461; L. D. Smith, "Land Laws of Tennessee," *Tennessee Law Review*, III (1924-25), 101-104.

38. Caldwell, *Sketches*, p. 298.

Chapter IV. Permanency in the New England Clergy: The General Problem and the New Hampshire Case

1. Essex North Association, *Contributions to the Ecclesiastical History of Essex County, Mass.* (Boston, 1865), pp. 22-23, 29-39; *Report on Congregationalism, Including a Manual of Church Discipline* (Boston, 1846), p. 29; Joseph S. Clark, *A Historical Sketch of the Congregational Churches in Massachusetts* (Boston, 1858), p. 228; Preston Cummings, *A Dictionary of Congregational Usages and Principles*, rev. ed. (Boston, 1853), s.v. "license"; Joseph Allen, *The Worcester Association and Its Antecedents* (Boston, 1868), pp. 17, 26-27.

2. Emil Oberholzer, Jr., *Delinquent Saints* (New York, 1956), esp. pp. 32-34.

3. Amherst (N.H.) Congregational Church, Records (typescript), p. 49, New Hampshire Historical Society, Concord.

4. Samuel Lee, *A Historic Discourse: Delivered at the Centennial Celebration of the First Congregational Church in New Ipswich, October 22, 1860* (Manchester, N.H., 1861), p. 31.

5. *Ibid.*, p. 26.

6. Humphrey Moore, *A Sermon Preached December 31, 1821, at the Funeral of Rev. Jacob Burrap, D.D. Late Pastor of the Church in Merrimack, N.H.* (Amherst, N.H., 1822), p. 8. Compare the sense of narrow escape from disunity in David Osgood's congratulatory "Right Hand of Fellowship," in Jeremy Belknap, *A Sermon, Preached at the Installation of the Rev. Jedidiah Morse . . . in Charlestown* (Boston, 1789), pp. 31-32.

7. Henry J. Ware, *Memoirs of Rev. Noah Worcester* (Boston, 1844), pp. 32-33; Eliza Lee, *Memoirs of the Rev. Joseph Buckminster, D.D. and of his son, Rev. Joseph Stevens Buckminster* (Boston, 1849), pp. 28-33, 355, 358. Compare Nathan Parker, *A Discourse Occasioned by the Death of the Rev. Joseph Buckminster* (Portsmouth, 1812), p. 20: "In this part of our country, where divisions and animosities are breaking up our churches, the loss, which we are called to deplore, is no small calamity."

8. Henry S. Burrage, *A History of the Baptists in New England* (Philadelphia, 1894), pp. 23-24, 27, 29-30, 47, gives some early examples that seem to fit this interpretation.

9. Isaac Backus, *A History of New England, with Particular Reference to the Denomination of Christians Called Baptists,* 2nd ed. (Newton, Mass., 1871), II, 265-266, 305. Backus's history, originally published between 1777 and 1796, is itself a document in the reorientation of Baptist thought. Compare Ebenezer E. Cummings, *A Sermon, Preached Before the New Hampshire Baptist State Convention* (Concord, N.H., 1836), p. 10; Burrage, pp. 70, 80-87, 224-227, 287-288.

10. Stephen Chapin, *A Sermon at the Ordination of the Rev. Samuel Cook, over the Baptist Church and Society in Effingham, N.H.* (Portland, 1822), p. 26. Compare Phineas Cooke, *A Discourse Delivered in Saxton's Village, Rockingham, Vt. at the Ordination of Rev. Sereno Taylor, to the Work of an Evangelist. November 2, 1824* (Bellows Falls, 1824).

11. Wade Crawford Barclay, *Early American Methodism, 1769-1844* (New York, 1949), I, 138, 229-230; *Minutes of the Annual Conferences of the Methodist Episcopal Church, for the Years 1773-*

1828 (New York, 1840), pp. 110-111, 443-444, 468, 498, 532-533, 539, 566, 572.

12. John Wise, *A Vindication of the Government of New-England Churches,* ed. Perry Miller (Gainesville, Fla., 1958), pp. 90-93. Wise's treatise was first published in 1717.

13. *Thirty Important Cases Resolved with Evidence of Scripture and Reason.* [*Mostly,*] *by Several Pastors of Adjacent Churches Meeting in Cambridge, New-England* (Boston, 1699), p. 29. And see pp. 27-30, on "A Question. In what cases a Minister may leave his people?" Cotton Mather endorses and expands this discussion in the section on "translation" of pastors in his *Ratio Disciplinae Fratrum Nov-Anglorum* (Boston, 1726), pp. 167-172.

14. Mather, *Ratio Disciplinae,* p. 169.

15. *Thirty Important Cases,* pp. 28, 30.

16. For a general discussion of these cases, see Henry Martyn Dexter, *The Congregationalism of the Last Three Hundred Years* (New York, 1880), pp. 504-507. Dexter, however, looking for vindication of his own ideas on pure Congregational polity, paid exclusive attention to those aspects of the late-eighteenth-century controversies that supported him.

17. [Esther K. Whitcomb and others], *History of Bolton, 1738-1938* (Bolton, Mass., 1938), pp. 66-67; Clifford K. Shipton, *Sibley's Harvard Graduates,* IX (Boston, 1956), 450-460; X (Boston, 1958), 175-185.

18. Nathaniel Whitaker, *A Confutation of Two Tracts . . . by the Rev. John Wise* (Boston, 1774), esp. pp. 9n, 10, 14, 16-17, 40-44.

19. [Ebenezer Chaplin], *A Treatise on Church Government . . . by a Neighbour* (Boston, 1773), esp. pp. 16-18, 20, 39; Ebenezer Chaplin, *A Second Treatise on Church Government* (Boston, 1773).

20. Zabdiel Adams, *The Happiness and Pleasure of Unity in Christian Societies* (Boston, 1772), esp. pp. 15, 27-30, 38-40; Zabdiel Adams, *Answer to a Pamphlet Lately Published Intitled "A Treatise on Church Government"* (Boston, 1773), pp. 32-35, 37-38, 66-67, 86.

21. *Observations upon the Congregational Plan of Church Government . . . by the Convention of Ministers of the Province of the Massachusetts-Bay* (Boston, 1773), pp. 8-9.

22. *Sundry Votes Passed by the Church of Christ in Dorchester, A.D. 1773. Previous to the Meeting of an Ecclesiastical Council There; with the Result of Said Council* (Boston, 1774), p. 18. Compare [Jonathan Bowman?], *Remarks on the Result of an Ecclesiastical Council, Which Met at Dorchester* (Boston, 1774), p. 38.

23. David Avery, *A Narrative of the Rise and Progress of the*

Difficulties Which Have Issued in a Separation between the Minister and People of Bennington, 1783 (Bennington, Vt., 1783), esp. pp. 32, 52.

24. Peter Thacher, *Observations upon the Present State of the Clergy of New-England, with Strictures upon the Power of Dismissing Them, Usurped by Some Churches* (Boston, 1783); James Sullivan, ¡*An Appeal to the Impartial Public, by the Society of Christian Independents, Congregating in Gloucester* (Boston, 1785), p. 15n. On the slightly later Matherian translation in Thacher's career, see William Buell Sprague, *Annals of the American Pulpit*, I (New York, 1857), 443, 719.

25. Thacher, *Observations*, pp. 8-9, 13.

26. [James Sullivan], *Strictures on the Rev. Mr. Thatcher's Pamphlet* (Boston 1784), pp. 4-5.

27. Thacher, *Observations*, pp. 3-4; [Sullivan], *Strictures*, pp. 6-17, 19-21, appendix pp. 1-2; Thacher, *A Reply to the Strictures of Mr. J. S.* (Boston, [1784]), pp. 11-12, 14.

28. Thacher, *Reply*, pp. 6-7.

29. *Ibid.*, p. 17.

30. *A Recommendation from the Convention of the Congregational Ministers, at Boston, May 26, 1790*, broadside; *Proceedings of the Convention of Congregational Ministers in the Commonwealth of Massachusetts* (Boston, 1795), pp. 14-15; Boston Association to "Rev. and Dear Sir," Boston, April 15th, 1799, broadside, Harvard College copy with MS endorsement by Jedidiah Morse; *An Address, from the Convention of Congregational Ministers in the Commonwealth of Massachusetts* [Boston, 1799].

31. Henry L. Shumway, "An Old-Time Minister," Worcester Society of Antiquity, *Collections*, XIX (1883), 45-67; Franklin Bowditch Dexter, *Biographical Sketches of the Graduates of Yale College*, III (New York, 1903), 13-17.

32. Ebenezer Chaplin, *That the Public May No Longer Be Imposed Upon by Party and Partial Reports, Concerning the Church and People in the Second Parish in Sutton, with Respect to Me, Ebenezer Chaplin, Their Pastor, My Office and Family* [n.p., 1793].

33. *Congregationalism, as Contained in the Scriptures, Explained by the Cambridge Platform . . . in a Series of Letters to a Gentleman from His Friend* (Boston, 1794), p. 15. Both Henry Martyn Dexter, *The Congregationalism of the Last Three Hundred Years*, appendix p. 168, and F. B. Dexter, *Biographical Sketches*, III, 16, attribute this pamphlet to Chaplin himself.

34. *Ibid.*, pp. 65-66.

35. *Piscataqua Evangelical Magazine*, I (1805), 7-8; Bernard A. Weisberger, *They Gathered at the River: The Story of the Great*

Revivalists and Their Impact upon Religion in America (Boston, 1958), p. 61, has some precise comments on the tensions in this orthodox revivalism.

36. "On the Trials of Ministers," *Piscataqua Evangelical Magazine,* IV (1808), 21-23.

37. "How We Congregationalists Treat Ministers," signed "Gaius," first came out in the Boston *Telegraph,* and was reprinted in *The Hopkinsian Magazine,* IV (1831), 9-13.

38. Moses Welch, "The Relations of Pastor and People," *Bibliotheca Sacra,* XII (1855), 30-31, 39, 47. Cf. E. N. Hidden, *A Sermon Preached at Chichester, N.H. Oct. 15, 1845, at the Ordination of Rev. Charles Willey* (Gilmanton, N.H., 1845), pp. 14-16.

39. N. Adams, "On Fulfilling the Ministry," *Bibliotheca Sacra,* III (1846), 753-755. Compare S. G. Bulfinch, "The Claims of the Ministry," *Christian Examiner,* XLIV (1848), 188, 192.

40. Daniel Dana, *The Importance of the Christian Ministry: A Sermon Preached before the American Society for Educating Youth for the Gospel Ministry, at Their Third Anniversary, Boston, Sept. 30, 1818* (Andover, Mass., 1818), pp. 21-22; see also p. 19.

41. John G. Palfrey, "An Address Delivered before the Society for Promoting Theological Education, June 5, 1831," *Christian Examiner,* XI (1831), 97.

42. "Ministerial Qualifications," signed "E.," *Spirit of the Pilgrims,* VI (1833), 269, 568.

43. William A. Stearns, "Education and Supply of Ministers in Different Ages and Countries," *Bibliotheca Sacra,* VIII (1851), 265.

44. "Thoughts on the Clerical Profession," signed "D.," *Religious Intelligencer,* I (1816-1817), 637-638; Heman Humphrey, "Duties of Ministers and People," *ibid.,* pp. 764-767, 778-781, 796-800; "Paulos" to the editor of the New York *Observer,* as reprinted in *Religious Intelligencer,* XXI (1836), 324-325.

45. David L. Parmelee, in *Proceedings of the North and South Consociations of Litchfield County, Ct. . . . to Commemorate the Centennial Anniversary of Their Primitive Organization* (Hartford, 1852), p. 36. Compare S. G. Bulfinch, "The Claims of the Ministry," *Christian Examiner,* XLIV (1848), p. 188.

46. Timothy Tuttle, "A Permanent Ministry," in *Contributions to the Ecclesiastical History of Connecticut; Prepared under the Direction of the General Association* (New Haven, 1861), pp. 239-240.

47. Nathaniel Bouton, *The Fathers of the New-Hampshire Ministry* (Concord, 1848), pp. 10-11.

48. Joseph H. Allen, "On Some Results of the Voluntary System,

Especially in Our Country Parishes," *Christian Examiner,* LXXXIV (1868), 207-229.

49. For the vague call to a new turn of mind, see especially Henry M. Dexter, "Pastorless Churches," *Minutes of the National Council of the Congregational Churches . . . 1877* (Boston, 1877), pp. 145-154.

50. *Minutes of the National Council . . . 1877,* pp. 408-409.

51. *Debates and Proceedings of the National Council, Held at Boston, Mass., June 14-24, 1865* (Boston, 1866), p. 3.

52. John N. McClintock, *History of New Hampshire* (Boston, 1888), pp. 527-528; George Barstow, *History of New Hampshire* (Concord, N.H., 1842), p. 432; *Constitution and Laws of the State of New Hampshire* (Dover, N.H., 1805), pp. 2, 393.

53. Thomas Shepard, "A Brief History of the Congregational Churches and Ministers in the State of Rhode Island," *American Quarterly Register,* XII (1839-40), 261-273.

54. Ebenezer E. Cummings, *A Sermon, Preached before the New-Hampshire Baptist State Convention, at Its Tenth Annual Meeting, Held at Deerfield, October 20, 1835* (Concord, N.H., 1836), pp. 41-45.

55. *Minutes of the National Council . . . 1877,* p. 416.

56. This high age at ordination brings into some question the old formula, "Five years from the Latin grammar to the pulpit." See Bouton, *The Fathers of the New Hampshire Ministry,* p. 9. Unless "pulpit" referred to the trial preaching that preceded ordination, the formula neglected a long gap bewteen the end of education and the beginning of the ministry.

57. "Churches and Ministers of Suffolk County," *American Quarterly Register,* VII (1834-35), 28-30.

58. *Congregational Quarterly,* III (1861), 84; VII (1865), 71; XVIII (1876), 128-129.

59. This picture emerges if, to the data in Henry A. Hazen, *The Congregational and Presbyterian Ministry and Churches of New Hampshire* (Boston, 1875), one adds data on large-town ministers from the *American Congregational Year-Book* for 1854 to 1859 (called the *Year Book of the American Congregational Union* in 1854); *Congregational Quarterly* for 1860 to 1878; *Congregational Year-Book* for later years; and from *Appleton's Cyclopedia of American Biography,* rev. ed. (New York, 1898), *sub* Zedekiah Smith Barstow, Nathaniel Bouton, Sarah Towne Marytn, William Jewett Tucker, and Jared Bell Waterbury.

60. See, for example, New Hampton Congregational Church Records, New Hampshire Antiquarian Society, Hopkinton, especially the dissolution entry of Nov. 13, 1833.

61. *A Remonstrance of the Congregational Church of Christ in Keene, N.H. against the Proceedings of the Town . . . Relative to*

the Pastor of Said Church (Bellows Falls, Vt., 1817), pp. 9-10. A similar sequence characterized New Ipswich, where many members left in the 1820's to join the Baptists or to move elsewhere, but where Samuel Lee survived as authoritarian pastor from 1836 to 1860; see New Ipswich Church Papers, New Hampshire Historical Society.

62. The generalizations in this section are based on examination of: (1) material by and about ministers of forty New Hampshire churches that experienced the "pure" pattern described (the ministers selected for study were those who served just before or just after the break in permanency; the materials were printed sermons, pamphlets, biographies, and local histories, plus some available manuscript correspondence and records); (2) official church, town, and parish records, available for some of the forty churches above and for other New Hampshire churches as well; (3) minutes of the Belknap, Harmony, Haverhill and Derry, Hollis, Hopkinton, and Manchester ministerial associations, of the Ecclesiastical Convention of the State of New Hampshire, and of the General Association of the Congregational and Presbyterian Churches of New Hampshire. Among these, the manuscript records are located primarily at the New Hampshire Historical Society, Concord.

63. Abraham Burnham, *A Sermon, Preached at the Installation of the Rev. Luke A. Spofford, in Brentwood, New-Hampshire, February 22, 1826* (Concord, 1826), p. 22.

64. For the construction of such a lie, compare the entries for Feb. 11 and Oct. 12, 1849, in Deerfield Congregational Church Records, New Hampshire Historical Society.

65. This tactic, based on the assumption of a right in continuous pastoral settlement, was used in New Hampshire as late as 1824; see Thomas Worcester, *A Few Serious Questions for Reason and Conscience to Decide: An Appeal to the Public, Occasioned by Proceedings of the Hopkinton Association, and by Recent Events in Salisbury* (Concord, 1824), p. 21.

66. Eleazar Wheelock, "To the Chh of Christ and Congregation of Gods People in Lebanon North Parish," 1766, MS, Dartmouth College Library 766900.1; Wheelock to Church and Congregation in Lebanon North Parish, June 6, 1769, Dartmouth College Library 769356; James Pinner and others to Legal Voters in Second Society in Lebanon, July 7, 1769, Dartmouth College Library 769407.1; Solo. Williams to Wheelock, July 13, 1769, Dartmouth College Library 769431.2; James Dow McCallum, *Eleazar Wheelock* (Hanover, N.H., 1939), pp. 39-56.

67. Belknap Association, Proceedings, Jan. 14, May 13, 1845, New Hampshire Historical Society.

68. Phineas Cooke, *Misapplication and Waste of Moral Power, A Sermon Delivered at the Installation of Rev. Stephen Morse, over the Congregational Church in Sharon, Vt., March 9, 1836* (Windsor, Vt., 1836), p. 13.

69. Elliott Colby Cogswell, *Memoirs of the Rev. Samuel Hidden* (Boston, 1842), pp. 127-130.

70. Samuel Lee, Statement read to Congregation of New Ipswich Church, Nov. 4, 1860; Results of "An Ecclesiastical Council . . . to consider the expediency of dissolving the pastoral relation between Rev. Samuel Lee and said Church," Dec. 4, 1860, and Calvin Cutler to Bro. Quimby, Jan. 29, 1862, New Ipswich Congregational Church Papers, New Hampshire Historical Society; Samuel Lee, *A Historic Discourse* (Manchester, N.H., 1861), pp. 61-78. Compare the account of the similarly forced resignation of Israel W. Putnam from Portsmouth North in 1835 in Lucius Harrison Thayer, *The Story of a Religious Democracy* (Portsmouth, N.H., 1921), pp. 32-33.

71. Stephen Chapin, *The Immoral Tendency of Error in Sentiment. A Farewell Sermon Delivered at Hillsborough, N.H., July 30, 1809* (Amherst, N.H., 1809).

72. Gilsum Church Records, p. 40 (May 16, 1830), New Hampshire Historical Society.

73. Transcript of Warner Congregational Church Records for 1771 and later years, in "Historical Collections," VA, 355-358, New Hampshire Antiquarian Society, Hopkinton.

74. Durham Congregational Church, Records, I, 2-4, 9, 16-17, 20, 27-28, 45-51, New Hampshire Historical Society.

75. Lee, *A Historic Discourse*, p. 53.

76. Nathan Lord to John Secombe and Others, March 25, 1823, Dartmouth College Library 823225.1.

77. Burnham, *A Sermon, Preached at the Installation of the Rev. Luke A. Spofford*, p. 16.

78. Isaac Hurd, Diary, ca. Dec. 15, 1816, New Hampshire Historical Society. Transcript of Records of Canaan Congregational Church, 1825, in "Historical Collections," II, 1, New Hampshire Antiquarian Society, Hopkinton; West Chester Presbyterian Parish, Records, Nov. 19, 1795, Jan. 28, 1833, New Hampshire Historical Society; Gilsum Church Records, Aug. 1, 1864, *ibid.*; Hebron Congregational Church Records, Feb. 21, 1833, *ibid.*

79. Francis Brown, *A Sermon, Delivered at Concord, New-Hampshire . . . before the Convention of Congregational and Presbyterian Ministers in Said State* (Concord, 1818), pp. 21-24. These ideas, which Brown expressed in relatively fresh language, soon became a routine part of local rhetoric; see, for example,

Notes on Sermon by John Kimball Young, 1837, in Almon Benson's Diary, vol. III, New Hampshire Historical Society.

80. See Nathaniel Bouton's acceptance of the ideas that ministers began to lose popularity after age fifty, whereas doctors and lawyers stayed in their prime into their seventies (Sermon read before the Derry and Manchester Association, ca. 1870, Bouton Papers, New Hampshire Historical Society).

81. This sequence, with the metropolis as the location of the mature stage, was familiar to Francis Brown as early as 1806. See George C. Shattuck to Francis Brown, Aug. 7, 1809, Dartmouth College Library 809457.

82. Joshua Bates, *A Sermon, Preached in Durham at the Ordination of the Rev. Federal Burt, June 18, 1817* (Dover, N.H., 1817).

83. Daniel Dana, *A Farewell Sermon Addressed to the First Presbyterian Church and Society in Newburyport, November 19, 1820* (Newburyport, Mass., 1820), pp. 3-5; Samuel Dana, *A Sermon Delivered at the Installation of the Rev. Daniel Dana, D.D. to the Pastoral Care of the West Presbyterian Church and Congregation in Londonderry, January 16, 1822* (Londonderry, N.H., 1822), p. 17; Daniel Dana, *A Discourse Delivered in the First Presbyterian Church in Newburyport, on Tuesday, Nov. 19, 1844, It Being the Fiftieth Anniversary of the Author's Ordination* (Newburyport, Mass., 1845), pp. 5, 21-23; W. C. Dana and others, *The Life of Daniel Dana* (Boston, 1866), pp. 98-133.

84. Hopkinton Association, Records, 1804-1840, New Hampshire Historical Society.

85. Charles Walker, Draft of Communication to Congregation, June 14, 1835, New Ipswich Congregational Church Papers, New Hampshire Historical Society, printed in Lee, *A Historic Discourse,* pp. 49-50.

86. "Report on Pastorless Churches and Churchless Pastors," *Minutes of the National Council . . . 1880* (Boston, 1880), pp. 129-130; Henry M. Dexter, "Pastorless Churches," *Minutes of the National Council . . . 1877,* pp. 145-54; Augustus F. Beard, "Undeveloped Power in Churches and in Individuals," *Minutes of the National Council . . . 1874* (Boston, 1875), p. 135; Edwards A. Park, "What Can Be Done for Augmenting the Number of Christian Ministers?" *Bibliotheca Sacra,* XXVIII (1871), pp. 88-90; Timothy Tuttle, "A Permanent Ministry," *Contributions to the Ecclesiastical History of Connecticut,* p. 245.

87. Preston Cummings, *A Dictionary of Congregational Usages and Principles,* rev. ed. (Boston, 1853); Henry Martyn Dexter, *The Congregationalism of the Last Three Hundred Years.* For contemporary comment on this historical awareness, see George B. Spalding,

Historical Discourse Delivered on the One Hundredth Anniversary of the Piscataqua Association of Ministers (Dover, N.H., 1881), esp pp. 33-34.

88. Edwards A. Park, *A Discourse Delivered in Boston before the Pastoral Association of Congregational Ministers in Massachusetts, May 28, 1844* (Andover, Mass, 1844), pp. 6, 8; see also pp. 5, 7, 10-15.

89. *A Letter to Professor Edwards A. Park . . . Touching His Late Sermon before the Pastoral Association of Massachusetts* (Boston, 1844).

90. [Committee on Congregationalism], *Report on Congregationalism, Including a Manual of Church Discipline* (Boston, 1846), pp. 29-30, 41.

91. *Debates and Proceedings of the National Council of Congregational Churches . . . 1865* (Boston, 1866), pp. 1-2, 7, 50-51, 147, 173, 222, 259-262, 276, 280-281, 309-310, 470, 489.

92. *Ibid.*, pp. 125-129. The longest single article of this section is not a description (or a prescription), but an argument for the "necessity for a recognized class of ministers, not holding office in any church" (p. 126).

93. *Ibid.*, p. 454.

94. *Minutes of the National Council . . . 1880* (Boston, 1880), pp. 119-130.

95. *Minutes of the National Council . . . 1877*, pp. 95-97.

96. *Minutes of the National Council . . . 1883* (Boston, 1883), pp. 18, 22, 26, 31; A. H. Quint, "Our Churches and Ministers," *ibid.*, pp. 54-60; "Report of Committee on Pastorate," *ibid.*, pp. 72-77; Report of Committee on Report of Committee of 1880 on the Pastorate," *ibid.*, pp. 161-163; "Report of the Committee on the Pastorate and Ministerial Standing," *Minutes of the National Council . . . 1886* (Boston, 1887), pp. 313-321.

97. "The Parish System," *Minutes of the National Council . . . 1877*, pp. 189-276; *Minutes of the National Council . . . 1880*, pp. 14-15, 61-76.

98. *Debates and Proceedings of the National Council . . . 1865*, p. 320.

99. *Minutes of the National Council . . . 1886*, pp. 43-44.

Chapter V. Stasis, 1850

1. John Bard to Samuel Bard, Jan. [17], 1764, Bard Papers, Bard College; Samuel Bard to John Bard, Dec. 29, 1762, Sept. 4, 1763; [1773], Bard Letters, New York Academy of Medicine; John Bard to Samuel Bard, April 9, 1763, *ibid.*

2. James J. Walsh, *History of Medicine in New York* (New York, 1919), I, 41.

3. Charles Warren, *A History of the American Bar* (Boston, 1911), pp. 86-87.

4. The basic materials on the convention are: *Journal of the Convention of the State of New York, Begun . . . June, 1846* (Albany, 1846); William G. Bishop and William H. Attree, *Report of the Debates and Proceedings of the Convention for the Revision of the Constitution of the State of New York, 1846* (Albany: Evening Atlas, 1846); S. Croswell and R. Sutton, *Debates and Proceedings in the New-York State Convention for the Revision of the Constitution* (Albany: *Argus*, 1846).

5. John W. Brown to D. D. Field, in "Law Reform in America," *Legal Observer*, XLIII (London, 1851-52), 273.

6. Compare, to the material in Bishop and Attree, p. 800, the tables of delegates' occupation, residence, and ancestry in Croswell and Sutton as well as in Bishop and Attree.

7. Henry Nicoll, in Bishop and Attree, p. 799; Charles O'Conor, in Croswell and Sutton, pp. 503-504.

8. George A. S. Crooker, in Croswell and Sutton, p. 46

9. Alfred Zantzinger Reed, *Training for the Public Profession of the Law* (New York, 1921), pp. 81-83, 88n; William Allen Butler, *Retrospect of Forty Years, 1825-1865*, ed. H. A. Butler (New York, 1911), 151; Rolls of Attorneys for 1846 and 1847, New York County Clerk's Office, Hall of Records, New York City.

10. *Journal of the Convention*, pp. 850-851. Croswell and Sutton, pp. 268-273.

11. Edwards A. Park, *A Discourse Delivered in Boston before the Pastoral Association of Congregational Ministers in Massachusetts, May 28, 1884* (Andover, Mass., 1844), p. 5.

12. [Cole,] *A Letter to Professor Edwards A. Park* (Boston, 1884).

13. Park, *Discourse*, pp. 5-6.

14. *Ibid.*, p. 7.

15. Henry Martyn Dexter, *The Congregationalism of the Last Three Hundred Years, as Seen in Its Literature* (New York, 1880), pp. 567-570; Gaius Glenn Atkins and Frederick L. Fagley, *History of American Congregationalism* (Boston and Chicago, 1942), pp. 360-362.

16. *Report on Congregationalism, Including a Manual of Church Discipline* (Boston, 1846), pp. 29-30; *Ecclesiastical Polity. The Government and Communion practised by the Congregational Churches in the United States of America Which Were Represented by Elders and Messengers in a National Council at Boston, A.D. 1865* (Boston, 1872), pp. 65-76.

17. Horace Green, MS Autobiography (1865), New York Academy of Medicine Library.

18. Philip Van Ingen, *A Brief Account of the First One Hundred Years of the New York Medical and Surgical Society* (Richmond, Va., 1946), pp. 38-44; *New York Medical and Surgical Reporter,* II (1847), 317-321.

19. John W. Francis, *An Inaugural Address. Delivered before the New-York Academy of Medicine, February 2d, 1848* (New York, 1848), 10.

20. L. R. Marsh to Green, July, 1855, [V. Mott] to Academy of Medicine, Jan. 19, 1859, H. C. Rutherford to Green, March 19, 1859, and Edmund Randolph Peaslee, In Memoriam (Eulogy on Green), New York Academy of Medicine Library; William Snow Miller, "Horace Green and His Probang," *Johns Hopkins Hospital Bulletin,* XXX (1919), 246-252.

21. *Medical News-Paper; or, the Doctor and the Physician* (Boston), vol. I (1822), *passim.*

22. Samuel A. Foot, *Autobiography* (New York, 1873), vol. I *passim;* Henry Watson Taft, *A Century and a Half at the New York Bar* (New York, 1938), pp. 28-29, 227-228.

23. Review of J. P. C. Sampson, *A Valedictory,* in H. Biglow's *American Monthly Magazine and Critical Review,* I (1817), 176; review of Charles Phillips, ed., *Specimens of Irish Eloquence,* in Charles K. Gardner's *Literary and Scientific Depository and Critical Review,* III (1812), 23-42.

24. George Templeton Strong, *Diary,* ed. Allan Nevins and Milton Halsey Thomas (New York, 1952), II, 478, IV, 282, 409, 487, 504.

25. Sir James Jay to James Duane, March 12, 1774, New-York Historical Society; John Watts to Robert Monckton, *Letter Book of John Watts,* New-York Historical Society Collections (New York, 1928), p. 255; Medical Society of the County of New York, Minutes, 1806-1830, New York Academy of Medicine Library; James R. Manley, in Medical Society of the State of New York, *Transactions . . . from Its Organization in 1807, up to and Including 1831* (Albany, 1868), pp. 390n, 391n, 393n; David Hosack, *Observations on the Establishment of the College of Physicians and Surgeons* (New York, 1811).

26. Samuel Bard to Francis U. Johnston, letters of 1817-1821, Columbia University Library; Henry U. Onderdonk to T. R. Beck, Nov. 6, 1813, Beck Letters, New York Public Library. For the publicly expressed hostility, see *New York Monthly Chronicle of Medicine and Surgery,* "Conducted by an Association of Physicians,"

I (1824-25). This attitude appeared commonly among physicians in all areas of the country; see John P. Harrison, *Essays and Lectures on Medical Subjects* (Philadelphia, 1835), p 191; John P. Harrison, *Moral Exposures of the Medical Profession* (Cincinnati, 1842), p. 5; John D. Goodman, "Professional Reputation," in *Addresses Delivered on Various Public Occasions* (Philadelphia, 1829), pp. 43-61; Ebenezer Alden, *An Address, Delivered in Hanover, N.H. before the Dartmouth Medical Society, on Their First Anniversary, December 28, 1819* (Boston, 1820), p. 5.

27. *Transactions of the Medical Society of the State of New-York, for the Year 1823, with an Appendix, Containing a System of Medcial Ethics* (New York, 1823), pp. 10, 20, 29. Contrast the virtual ignoring of advertising in two American adaptations of Percival's code, also in the 1820's: *Extracts from the Medical Ethics, or a Code of Institutes and Precepts, Adapted to the Professional Conduct of Physicians and Surgeons, in Private or General Practice* (Lexington, [Ky.], 1821); and *Extracts from the Medical Ethics of Dr. Percival* (Philadelphia, 1829). The first extension of this ban to cover any public reporting of cases was apparently stated by *A System of Medical Ethics, Adopted by the Medico-Chirurgical Society of Baltimore* (Baltimore, 1823), pp. 11-12.

28. For an unusually articulate description of these clubs as useful steps toward the fight by "a scientific socialism" against degrading "individualism," see Worthington Hooker, *Report of the [A.M.A.] Committee on Medical Education* (Philadelphia, 1851), pp. 22-23. See also Thomas Cock, *Inaugural Address, Delivered before the New York Academy of Medicine, April 7, 1852* (New York, 1852), pp. 15-22; Chauncey D. Leake, "A Gentleman Physician of New York: Dr. David Hosack," 1920, revised 1947, typescript in New York Academy of Medicine Library, p. 23; Philip Van Ingen, "Remarks on 'Kappa Lambda, Elf or Ogre,'" *Bulletin of the History of Medicine,* XVIII (1945), 513-538; J. L. Vandervoost, in *New York Journal of Medicine and Surgery,* I (1839), 204-209.

29. Samuel A. Seaman, *Annals of New York Methodism* (New York and Cincinnati, 1892), pp. 215-231, 266-275; New York Annual Conference, Journals, May 17, 1839, Methodist Episcopal Church Papers, New York Public Library; Association of Local Preachers of the Methodist Episcopal Church for Mutual Improvements, Minutes, 1842-1843, *ibid.;* Trustees' letter, 1813, in Minutes of Leaders Meeting 1811-1823, *ibid.;* Trustees of the Methodist Episcopal Church, New York, Minutes, July 1, 1829, Sept. 1, 1830, April 6, May 4, 1831, Jan. 20, Feb. 20, March, 6, 1833, Jan. 1, 8, 29, 1834, *ibid.;* John Guion to Bishop Hobart, May 1, 1813, Samuel Haskell

to Hobart, May 31, Aug. 25, 1813, Samuel F. Jarvis to Hobart, June 15, September 1813, Hobart Papers, Church Historical Society, Austin, Texas.

30. The crucial nature of this test was recognized implicitly in S. W. Butler, *Doctors' Commons: An Ethic Address, Delivered before the District Medical Society, for the County of Burlington* (Burlington, [N.J.], 1854), p. 6: "Exterior harmony is in entire accordance with the unshackled maintenance of individuality." The context shows that Butler, mouthing this precept, felt some need to convince his audience.

31. *United States Medical and Surgical Journal*, II (1835-36), 208.

32. See Richard D. Birdsall, *Berkshire County: A Cultural History* (New Haven, 1959), chs. 9 and 10.

Index

and fees, 4-5; "free-lance," 5; and Great Awakening, 11, 95; "hireling," 1, 2, 5; historical concept, 169-170; and Hopkinton Association, 168-169; Methodist, itinerant, 89, 94, 116; novelty in, 108, 152; primacy of, 15; professionalism in, 170-171, 174; rural, 157; tasks, 2, 90-91. *See also* Permanency; Tenure

Missionaries, 107, 169, 172, 173

Monopoly: and clergy, 89-90; fear of, 7, 9, 12; of legal practice, 67, 78; medical, 13, 52-54. *See also* Competition

Montgomery County, N.Y., 30

Moores, J. B., 81

Morris, Gouverneur, 25

Mott, Valentine, 185

Nativism, 182, 183, 189

Nature healing, 3

Navy, 28

Newburyport, Mass., 168

New England: "feeble" churches, 112-113, 114, 149; frontier, 13, 107, 126-128, 132, 160, 166, 170, 175; missions to, 107-108; organic community, 128-130; and pastoral relation, 172; rural economic decline, 113, 115, 158-162, 166, 167

New Hampshire Association of Ministers, 118

New Hampshire, ministerial permanence in, 116-167

New Ipswich, N.H., 162, 164, 169

New York Academy of Medicine, 20, 22, 44, 50, 185; and Horace Green, 52; origins, 40-41

New York Constitutional Convention (1846), 180-182

New York County Medical Society, *see* Medical Society of the County of New York

New York Dispensary, 28-29, 43

New York Hospital, 28, 34; medical library, 43

New York medical community, 20-58, 179; composition, 38-40; and group size, 31, 35, 37-43, 50; and

policy formulation, 36-37; schisms, 26-37; and upstate physician, 29-31

New York Medical and Surgical Society (1839), 42, 51; and group size, 43; and Horace Green, 52, 185

New York School of Medicine, 38-39

News, medical, and anomymity, 200n12

Nostrum venders, 22

O'Conor, Charles, 181, 189

Oldcastle, John, *see* Benton

Oliphant, David, 158

Ordination, ministerial, 133, 147; age at, 140, 142, 214n56; bureaucratic, 184; of missionaries, 169

Organicism: and circuit bar, 62; and community, 128-130, 170; and pastoral relation, 88-89, 100. *See also* Localism

Organization, professional, 7-9; alumni, 42; and group cohesion, 8, 14; and jealousy, 50; medical, 17, 26, 27, 28, 37, 41, 42-43, 50, 52, 53-54; and militia, 17; of ministers, 95, 104; and regulation, 13, 178. *See also* Associations; Group; Societies

Orthodoxy, 15

Overton, John, 70-71

Palfrey, John G., 111

Panics (1837, 1839), *see* Depression

Parish, 103, 106, 174, 175, 176; destitute, 166, 168; lands, 113

Park, Edwards A., 170-171; privatism of, 182-184

Parsons' Cause (Virginia), 162

Partnerships, legal, 78-79, 82

Pastor: "acting," 175-176; "colleague," 91, 162; and community solidarity, 92; and congregation, 108; definition in Cambridge Platform, 171; and economics, 98-99; literary demands on, 109; salaried, 2, 91-92; security of